My Lord's Money

MY LORD'S MONEY

Or, the Consecration of Talents

Ernest Boys and Boys

Waymark Books
Cedar Lake, Michigan

Copyright ©2020 Waymark Books

Waymark Books
P.O. Box 7
Cedar Lake, MI 48812-0007

www.waymarkbooks.com

ISBN #978-1611047899

CONTENTS

Preface		vii
1.	My Talents, His Money	1
2.	The Definite Consecration of Talents	6
3.	Life, a Talent	14
4.	Influence as Talent	20
5.	Social Position	29
6.	Educational Advantages	38
7.	Musical Gifts	44
8.	The Consecrated Pen	51
9.	Money as a Talent	63
10.	Time as a Talent	72

PREFACE

The present volume is intended as a sequel to one already published, entitled *The Consecrated Life*. The numerous letters received by the author expressing thankfulness for help received from that book, encourages him to pursue the subject further.

The life of consecration to God is indeed a wide and comprehensive subject. To exhaust it is well-nigh impossible. As the questions arise in one's mind, one by one, which must occur in the daily life of those who desire to be really consecrated to God, it seems difficult to select a few out of the many for detailed consideration.

The author hopes that those which he has selected for the present volume (which are the result of considerable personal acquaintance with the difficulties besetting the Christian life) will be found useful to many towards settling any questions or difficulties which may be present, and also towards stirring up all his readers to a more diligent use of the talents committed to their trust.

He has endeavored to treat the various subjects in the most practical manner, and to throw out suggestions which all his readers can apply to themselves, with such modifications as their special circumstances in life may require.

Those who find the book helpful are invited, first of all, to thank God for it; and then, if they will, to send a line to the author specially naming the particular difficulty which has been met. This will be a help to him in such future works as the Lord permits him to write.

All who find the volume of use are also invited to make it known, as much as possible, to others.

Ernest Boys
Beverly, Sidcup, Kent

1

MY TALENTS, HIS MONEY

In a previous volume[1] by the present writer, the subject of consecration to God has been somewhat fully handled. The general principles, however, of consecration, and the application of these to those various conditions of outward life in which all are more or less equally involved, was the line followed out. Very little was said in detail about the consecrating to God of those powers, and faculties of mind and body, with which we are endowed, nor of the definite dedication to Him of the more individual and personal circumstances in which we are each placed. In these one differs so much from another, that what may be said of one person would not always refer in the same measure to all alike. And yet the subjects must be so treated that each may recognize some method of "doing the will of God from the heart,' in those individual and personal circumstances. This is the work which the writer proposes, with God's blessing, now to undertake.

1. The Consecrated Life. The little volume may be ordered of any bookseller. It is published by Messrs Nisbet and Co., 21 Berners Street, London, W.

All that we shall have to say in this volume will relate to what are generally called "talents." This word has come to be applied to all that God has committed to our charge to be used for Him; and it has therefore a very wide range of application. It has been so applied, of course, from its use in our Lord's well-known parable related to Matthew 25:14-30.

The parable was spoken in reference to His Second Advent. He likens His return to that of a master from a long journey, who at once asks of his servants an account of money which he had entrusted to their care, for use in trading during his absence. The usual interpretation, that these talents represent the various graces, gifts, and opportunities with which we are entrusted, is no doubt the right one; and we cannot help thinking that we may very profitably consider the consecration of these to the service of God from this point of view. We shall not, however, deal with those endowments which we usually speak of as Christian graces; but we shall confine our attention to the natural gifts of mind and body, and the opportunities of usefulness within our reach.

Before entering into detail as regards a few of these, we must recollect some very essential truths which are common to all alike, and which may be gathered from the parable of the talents.

And firstly, we must think of them all as represented by a sum of *money*; there is much to be learned as to their value and their use.

Money has a specific value of its own, settled by common consent, and not left to each one's judgment to determine. It is, as regards itself, as valuable in the hands of those inexperienced in its use, as in those of the merchant who trades with it successfully. It is just as precious whether its value is known or not. But where its value is not understood, there is loss to the owner, and to those to whom it might have been made of use. So it is surely with all our talents. They have their value, and an unspeakable value it is. This is quite apart from any opinion we may form of them. Their value is in themselves. Whether recognized or not, it remains the same. But where it is not recognized, serious loss is sure to follow both to the owner, and to the many who might have been benefited by them.

But further, money is not only of value in itself, it is also for use.

In the parable, all but the slothful servant "traded" with it. However great its value, considered only in itself, it is perfectly unproductive unless use is made of it. Indeed, unused, nothing is more useless. Thousands of pounds locked up and put away are of no use to anyone. Their owner cannot enjoy them. He might just as well be without them. But, on the other hand, nothing so repays the using of it as money. Put out to use, it is capable of steady increase. Money used makes more money. And not only does it multiply itself; but it is capable also of producing an endless variety of most useful results. It is so also with all our talents. Their usefulness depends not upon their intrinsic value, but upon the use which we make of them. Neglected or unused, they fail to produce their proper results. Used, they increase by exercise and experience; they literally multiply themselves. And over and above this, there is no end to the blessed and happy results which flow out to others on every side of us, when our talents are rightly employed.

And this brings us to another most important consideration. In using money, it is most essential to use it *to the very best advantage*. We mean by this much more than merely using it well, as distinguished from making a bad use of it. There are many ways of making a good use of it; and some yield a more profitable return than others. The right use of money is an art, which requires thought and study. It must be laid out in the best markets, in the best way, and at the best time.

The same amount of money will do much more in some people's hands than in others'. From one point of view, both might be said to make a good use of it; but from another point of view one of them makes a much better use of it than the other. So, again, it is with all our talents. Among those who endeavor to use them well, some make so much more than the others. Some scarcely seem to know how to use them at all. Some who have much more talents than others make far less mark with them, simply from not using them rightly. Talents of all sorts should be laid out to the very best advantage, so as to secure the largest possible returns.

And this thought leads us on to another which is equally important. The best use must be made of our talents, for the simple reason that they *are not our own*. In the most solemn sense they are entrusted to us. They are like the master's money in the parable, which was entrusted to his servants to employ *for him*, just because it was actually *his*, and not their own.

Even the unprofitable servant, who made no use of it, still recognized that it was his master's, and not his own, money (Matthew 25:25). And the master so distinctly recognized it as his property, once calling it 'my money,' and once 'mine own' (verse 26). But we are so slow even to recognize all our talents as not our own, but belonging to the Master. We take credit for them, and accept praise for them, and forget to hand on all praise and credit untouched by us to Him. Nay, we sometimes feed our own pride by dwelling upon the points wherein we may excel another, as if our talents were the produce of our own abilities and efforts. And in our use of them, we too often have our own aims in view, instead of endeavoring to discover what He would have us do. Very often to satisfy a conscience which would not be at rest, if they were not employed at all, we lay them out just anyhow, instead of thoughtfully considering how we may do so to the very best possible advantage. All this arises from forgetfulness that they are 'our Lord's money.'

Hence arises the need of a very real consecration of them to Him. And in doing so, let us remember the great secret of all the believer's consecration, which is clearly to recognize that all absolutely and really belongs to Him already, whether we have recognized it or not.[2] Consecration is not an act on our part, making anything His which was not just as really His before. It is simply the practical and sustained recognition that it does so belong to Him, and must therefore be used only in His service. The talent of the unprofitable servant, wrapped in the napkin, and buried in the earth, was just as truly 'his Lord's money' as if he had been using it for his master. The consecration of the other two servants was not any act of theirs by which they made over the money to him, for it was his already, but

---

2. This view of the subject, in its bearing on the believer's personal consecration to God, is fully explained in The Consecrated Life, pp. 15 to 18.

merely the recognition of his ownership over it, and the using of it accordingly for him.

2

THE DEFINITE CONSECRATION OF TALENTS

In a previous volume[1] by the present writer, the subject of consecration to God has been somewhat fully handled. The general principles, however, of consecration, and the application of these to those various conditions of outward life in which all are more or less equally involved, was the line followed out. Very little was said in detail about the consecrating to God of those powers, and faculties of mind and body, with which we are endowed, nor of the definite dedication to Him of the more individual and personal circumstances in which we are each placed. In these one differs so much from another, that what may be said of one person would not always refer in the same measure to all alike. And yet the subjects must be so treated that each may recognize some method of "doing the will of God from the heart," in those individual and personal

---

1. The Consecrated Life. The little volume may be ordered of any bookseller. It is published by Messrs Nisbet and Co., 21 Berners Street, London, W.

circumstances. This is the work which the writer proposes, with God's blessing, now to undertake.

All that we shall have to say in this volume will relate to what are generally called "talents." This word has come to be applied to all that God has committed to our charge to be used for Him; and it has therefore a very wide range of application. It has been so applied, of course, from its use in our Lord's well-known parable related to Matthew 25:14-30.

The parable was spoken in reference to His Second Advent. He likens His return to that of a master from a long journey, who at once asks of his servants an account of money which he had entrusted to their care, for use in trading during his absence. The usual interpretation, that these talents represent the various graces, gifts, and opportunities with which we are entrusted, is no doubt the right one; and we cannot help thinking that we may very profitably consider the consecration of these to the service of God from this point of view. We shall not, however, deal with those endowments which we usually speak of as Christian graces; but we shall confine our attention to the natural gifts of mind and body, and the opportunities of usefulness within our reach.

Before entering into detail as regards a few of these, we must recollect some very essential truths which are common to all alike, and which may be gathered from the parable of the talents.

And firstly, we must think of them all as represented by a sum of *money*; there is much to be learned as to their value and their use.

Money has a specific value of its own, settled by common consent, and not left to each one's judgment to determine. It is, as regards itself, as valuable in the hands of those inexperienced in its use, as in those of the merchant who trades with it successfully. It is just as precious whether its value is known or not. But where its value is not understood, there is loss to the owner, and to those to whom it might have been made of use. So it is surely with all our talents. They have their value, and an unspeakable value it is. This is quite apart from any opinion we may form of them. Their value is in themselves. Whether recognized or not, it remains the same. But where it is not recognized, serious loss is sure to follow both to the owner, and to the many who might have been benefited by them.

But further, money is not only of value in itself, it is also for use. In the parable, all but the slothful servant "traded" with it. However great its value, considered only in itself, it is perfectly unproductive unless use is made of it. Indeed, unused, nothing is more useless. Thousands of pounds locked up and put away are of no use to anyone. Their owner cannot enjoy them. He might just as well be without them. But, on the other hand, nothing so repays the using of it as money. Put out to use, it is capable of steady increase. Money used makes more money. And not only does it multiply itself; but it is capable also of producing an endless variety of most useful results. It is so also with all our talents. Their usefulness depends not upon their intrinsic value, but upon the use which we make of them. Neglected or unused, they fail to produce their proper results. Used, they increase by exercise and experience; they literally multiply themselves. And over and above this, there is no end to the blessed and happy results which flow out to others on every side of us, when our talents are rightly employed.

And this brings us to another most important consideration. In using money, it is most essential to use it *to the very best advantage*. We mean by this much more than merely using it well, as distinguished from making a bad use of it. There are many ways of making a good use of it; and some yield a more profitable return than others. The right use of money is an art, which requires thought and study. It must be laid out in the best markets, in the best way, and at the best time.

The same amount of money will do much more in some people's hands than in others'. From one point of view, both might be said to make a good use of it; but from another point of view one of them makes a much better use of it than the other. So, again, it is with all our talents. Among those who endeavor to use them well, some make so much more than the others. Some scarcely seem to know how to use them at all. Some who have much more talents than others make far less mark with them, simply from not using them rightly. Talents of all sorts should be laid out to the very best advantage, so as to secure the largest possible returns.

And this thought leads us on to another which is equally important. The best use must be made of our talents, for the simple reason that they *are not our own*. In the most solemn sense they are entrusted to us. They are like the master's money in the parable, which was entrusted to his servants to employ *for him*, just because it was actually *his*, and not their own.

Even the unprofitable servant, who made no use of it, still recognized that it was his master's, and not his own, money (Matthew 25:25). And the master so distinctly recognized it as his property, once calling it 'my money,' and once 'mine own' (verse 26). But we are so slow even to recognize all our talents as not our own, but belonging to the Master. We take credit for them, and accept praise for them, and forget to hand on all praise and credit untouched by us to Him. Nay, we sometimes feed our own pride by dwelling upon the points wherein we may excel another, as if our talents were the produce of our own abilities and efforts. And in our use of them, we too often have our own aims in view, instead of endeavoring to discover what He would have us do. Very often to satisfy a conscience which would not be at rest, if they were not employed at all, we lay them out just anyhow, instead of thoughtfully considering how we may do so to the very best possible advantage. All this arises from forgetfulness that they are 'our Lord's money.'

Hence arises the need of a very real consecration of them to Him. And in doing so, let us remember the great secret of all the believer's consecration, which is clearly to recognize that all absolutely and really belongs to Him already, whether we have recognized it or not.[2] Consecration is not an act on our part, making anything His which was not just as really His before. It is simply the practical and sustained recognition that it does so belong to Him, and must therefore be used only in His service. The talent of the unprofitable servant, wrapped in the napkin, and buried in the earth, was just as

---

2. This view of the subject, in its bearing on the believer's personal consecration to God, is fully explained in The Consecrated Life, pp. 15 to 18.

truly 'his Lord's money' as if he had been using it for his master. The consecration of the other two servants was not any act of theirs by which they made over the money to him, for it was his already, but merely the recognition of his ownership over it, and the using of it accordingly for him.

Having pressed the necessity of the consecration of our talents to God 'being very real,' we must next clearly point out that, in order to bring this about, it must be very *definite*; and we shall now endeavor to make some suggestions which may help towards effecting this.

We must as far as possible discover what our talents are. Some are in a measure common to all alike. Others are more special; and these are not equally bestowed upon those who possess them. Some may have few talents; others many: but none are without any, from the least to the greatest. 'Every man,' in the parable, received something from the master (verse 15). Many hardly recognize what talents they have. They have so often thought of such things as riches, health, and high station in life, as talents, but have never looked upon poverty, sickness, low estate, and many other things in which they have a share, in the same light. But as a matter of fact, everything is a talent that we can use in God's service, to bring glory to Him, and to advance His kingdom in the world. This view enlarges very much the list of everyone's talents, and opens up avenues of definite service, where were before unrecognized. We hope in these papers to make this plain to all.

Having discovered and recognized our talents, the next thing is not to underrate them. Some cannot do this. Their special gifts and opportunities are so obvious, that it would be simple affectation to speak lightly of them. Such people, however, often need a more lively sense of their responsibility.

But others are tempted to underestimate their talents. Because these are not brilliant and obvious, they think they have very little entrusted to them, and can accomplish next to nothing. These people also need to be awakened to a careful use of their little. They are in danger of hiding their Lord's money. And it is remarkable that in the parable to the man who did so was the one to whom least was entrusted. Supposing, however, that their talent *is* small, it is as important to be 'faithful in a very little' (Luke 19:17) as in the greater gifts. But as a matter of fact, we cannot estimate how great or little they are.

God requires the talents of each of us in the sphere in which we have been placed. Compared with the heavenly rewards for their right employment, it is true that they are all regarded as 'a few things' (Matthew 25:21, 23), and 'a very little' (Luke 19:17). But considered in themselves, they are all of equal importance for the sphere in which they are needed, and for which they are given to us by God. They are not measured out to 'every man' *anyhow*, but 'according to his several ability' (verse 15), a very comforting expression.

The abilities of each individual are duly considered in the bestowment of them. Talents not needed are not bestowed. But those which are given will most surely find a sphere of exercise close at hand, if it is only recognized.

From this point of view, no single talent is of little value. 'The Lord hath need of it' makes all the difference. That made the obscure young colt on that special occasion, when prophecy had to be fulfilled, even more necessary than the finest horse in Palestine. And it is exactly so with our talents. Wherever God needs them they are of the very first importance. The talents of the humblest cottager are more needed in his cottage home than the brilliant gifts of the statesman or the preacher; and *there* they are far more important. The same is true of every condition of life.

Then, it is so necessary definitely to regard our talents as very real openings for the direct service of God. This is as true of talents which relate to the ordinary and daily surroundings of life, as of those which refer to what is more usually called 'religious' work. It is as true of the talents employed in making home life all it ought to be, as of those needed for preaching the Gospel, or for writing books on spiritual life for thousands to read. If the 'Lord hath need' of both, He is served as much by one as the other. The one may produce results bearing more directly on eternity; but all are for Him.

The routine of domestic employment, or of the necessary business of life, are avenues through which our talents may do Him service, none the less than preaching and teaching in church, if our whole life is devoted to His glory.³ The recollection of this will surround the most ordinary and 'humdrum' life with splendid and constant possibilities of serving God.

And lastly, a word about the responsibility for our talents, and the reward for the right use of them. It will stimulate to increased diligence, and to more definite consecration.

Never let us forget that we are responsible for our talents. They are not only for use, but God *expects* us to use them, and will require an account of them. We so easily forget this account to be rendered, just because we so often forget that they are not our own, but *His*. If they are His, *of course* an account must be rendered for each of them. None can be left out of His reckoning, however much we may have left them out of ours. The unused talent of the slothful servant was brought into the account, just as much as those which had been usefully employed by the others.

Let us remember then that, at the judgment seat of Christ, when He comes again, this account must be rendered by everyone. Day by day, and hour by hour, we are laying up the materials for that searching judgment; and so our whole life's work is bound up very solemnly with the Second Advent. We are trading now with our Lord's money, and on His return He will 'reckon' with servants (verse 19) to 'know how much every man had gained by trading' (Luke 19:15). The reckoning is to be as *individual* as the bestowment of the talents is: and proportionate results will be expected from their use.

But then comes the grand reward. It is very solemn to bear in mind that, apart from the question of personal salvation through faith in Christ, the rewards of His future kingdom are to be proportioned according to *works*. 'My reward is with Me, to give to every man according as His work shall be' (Revelation 22:12), is just

---

3. Further teaching on this point will be found in the chapter entitled 'Consecration in Daily Life,' in The Consecrated Life. Readers are referred to it for thoughts, which space forbids to be repeated here.

as true as, 'By grace you are saved through faith…not of works, lest any man should boast' (Ephesians 2:8-9).

The reconciliation is to distinguish between salvation itself, and the rewards which will be given to the saved according to the measure of their works. And we may safely say that the whole question of works centers round the right employment of the talents entrusted to us. These are the tools with which we are to work, and these indicate the sort of work we are intended to do. But the actual amount of reward will depend upon how earnestly we do the work. Each day we live we are in this solemn way making our mark upon eternity.

In regard, then, to all the talents entrusted to us, let us be 'always abounding in the work of our Lord, knowing that our labor is not in vain in the Lord' (1 Corinthians 15:58).

3

LIFE, A TALENT

After the introductory remarks already made with regard to the nature and reality of consecration, as applied to the talents which God has entrusted us, we shall now pass on to consider in detail several of the talents themselves. We hope to throw out practical suggestions which may help our readers to such an employment of their various talents, as shall most bring glory to God, and secure for them the full measure of reward, when the Master 'reckons with them,' in order to 'know how much every man has gained by trading.'

We shall commence with one talent which seems to comprehend all the rest; but we shall try to say enough about it to be useful and suggestive, without anticipating what will remain to be said about others. Yet at the same time, much that we shall write in the present chapter will refer also, in some measure, to almost all that follow. And as we shall not be able constantly to repeat the same thoughts, whenever it may seem called for, we must ask our readers very carefully to weigh what we shall now put before them, and to bear it in mind throughout succeeding chapters.

We shall first, then, consider LIFE in the light of a talent committed to our care. This is going directly to the root of the whole matter, and touches a subject which some who try to number up their talents may have passed over without notice, or at all events without the careful consideration it requires.

Life, considered in itself, is an unspeakably mysterious and sacred thing. It is so specially a manifestation of the Being of God Himself,—the great Source of all life. This is as true of every form of animal and vegetable life, down to the very lowest type of it, as it is of human life. That wonderful and hidden power, at work on every side of us, which we call Nature, is none other than the Life of God, manifesting itself through millions of different channels.

Life, in whatever form it appears, speaks to all who have ears to hear of the Almighty Living One, who is the Source and Support of it all. God Himself is the very essence of life; but of all the forms in which His life is exhibited in the works of His hands, next to the angelic beings, man is the highest and the noblest, the nearest to God. Therefore, it is a solemn thing to live.

The possession, then, of life brings the creature into closer, more definite, and more sustained relationship with God, than that which exists between Him and His inanimate creation. We may truly say, that all things which have life, are in a deeper and more special way, *His very own*, being linked to Him by the life-principle which they possess, an which He every moment sustains.

From this point of view, the human family, in which is exhibited more fully than in all other earthly creatures the Life of God, so specially belong to Him. This is true of all mankind, quite apart from the question of conversion to God. And it shows us so clearly the position of those who are living, whether under a Christian profession or not, for self, for the world, and for sin. We have the whole principle of consecration taught us thus from purely natural religion; and we have God's claim upon the hearty service of all mankind, in its very simplest, but most undeniable, form.

But there are other reasons why Life should be viewed by us as a most precious talent, besides the fact that it brings us into such special connection with God and makes us so peculiarly His very own.

Not only is Life such a mysterious and solemn thing in itself, but our bodily organs have such a mysterious hold upon it; and a very slender hold it is. So little is needed to loosen it: and its continuance is a daily reminder of our entire dependence upon the will of God for every moment of the Life we live. Thus while Life in its commencement brings us into such close relationship with God, and *makes* us very specially His; so Life in its continuance each moment *keeps* us entirely His own.

Moreover, Life is a talent of very precious value, because, once lost, it is gone for good, so far as this present world is concerned. And in connection with this thought, we would press upon the Christian the absolute duty not only of using the great talent of Life, so long as it is entrusted to him, to the very fullest advantage, but also of taking every proper means for preserving as long as possible the use of it. In other words, we regard it as essential to true consecration to God, that we take due care of the Life which He has entrusted to us, and which is so really His.

We insist upon this, because so many lose sight of it. Admitting that their Life is not their own, they yet fail to see that they must not only possess and use it for God, but also *preserve* it for Him. And since the preservation of Life depends upon the observance of all the conditions of health, we must look to it very carefully that we do not neglect them.

Unhealthy habits of every kind, late hours, hurried meals, bad air, neglected exercise, overwork, tight dressing, exposure to cold and damp, giving way to violent emotions, or to wearying anxiety, indeed, all that exhausts unduly the nervous energy, or taxes too heavily the strength, tends to shorten Life, and reduces the period during which we may use this talent for God upon earth.

And not only should these matters be attended to for the sake of prolonging and preserving the talent of Life itself; but they are equally essential for a full and useful employment of the talent during the time we possess it. We mean that the Christian who observes, as far as may be, the conditions of health, and thus preserves the highest possible vigor of mind and body, is able to take up spheres of work which are not open to invalids. While it is true that there is a special talent in bodily weakness (when its patient endurance brings glory to God), a talent which may be most really laid out for God, yet the fact remains that vigorous Life is the most favorable condition for promoting the kingdom of Christ.

A few other considerations remain which all serve to remind us how precious is the talent of Life.

The preciousness of Life is enhanced by its very uncertainty. And this is another of the mysteries of Life. No one can promise himself a single day. A few days' sickness may carry off many who seem in tolerable health. A momentary accident may remove the healthiest and strongest. And while it is a solemn duty, from the human standpoint, to preserve health, yet those who seek to do so do not always live longer than those who do not. But the practical conclusion from all this uncertainty is, that Life, while it lasts, is all the more precious because of it. And the Christian, who cannot look in advance to be *absolutely sure* of its continuance, will see that each day, as he lives it out hour by hour, is not only not wasted, but turned to the highest account. He will endeavor to follow the admirable rule of living each day as if it were his last.

But over and above the uncertainty of Life, and the possibility of an early decease, we think that the preciousness of this talent is increased also by its very shortness, however, long it may happen to be. Granting us even the full length of possible existence, it is after all short enough, and less than a moment when compared with eternity. This is the view of Life which we prefer to urge, whether we are exhorting the unconverted to repent and believe, or the converted to a more earnest Life of service to God. We like to make it clear, that, while the possibility of early death is an argument of great force, yet apart from this, there is no time to lose, even in the very longest Life.

And this appears all the more forcible when we remember that the longest Life is naturally divided into shorter portions, which are very rapidly passing away. Each of these brings with it some special opportunities connected with that particular period of Life, which much be made use of at the right time, or else for the most part they are lost altogether.

The periods of childhood, of school life, of young manhood and young womanhood, of entering professions, of marriage, of parental responsibilities, of middle age, of old age, have all their peculiar openings for God's service.[1] Indeed, each day and each hour of the longest Life brings with it its own opportunities, which must be made use of at the moment. And from this point of view, also, the 'threescore years and ten,' or even the 'fourscore years' seem short enough; and there is no period which we can afford to lose for God.

And once more, these considerations about the preciousness of Life are still further strengthened, when we remember that the service which we can now render to God is so peculiarly connected with this present world, and one which, as far as we know, can only be rendered to Him through our personal agency. Whatever may be the happy services with which ' His servants shall serve Him ' (Revelation 22:3) in the eternal state, it will be of a somewhat different sort to our present earthly service. We are now privileged to witness for Him and His truth in a world of darkness. We are to be 'the salt of the earth,' and the 'light of the world' (Matthew 13, 14).

We are to be the instruments of His own use in bringing souls to salvation. It is a work which angels might long to do; but it is given to us. And Life is the grand opportunity for its accomplishment: for with Life it must cease.

While we ponder then these things, let us rise to a truer view of the responsibility under which Life places us. Let the easygoing, idle, self-indulgent Christian (and there are plenty such) see at once the privilege and the duty of having a real aim in Life. Let that purposeless, aimless Life, which so many live, be a thing of the past. Let us see that to live at all is an intensely solemn thing. And in view of the account which we must render of this most precious talent, let us take care that we do not lay it up in a napkin, hiding our Lord's money in the earth. Rather let us freely use it in His service, that at His coming He may receive *His own* with usury.

Are any of our readers unconverted? Are any who believe

---

1. These ideas will be developed in a future chapter on Influence. It is enough just to suggest them now for further thought.

themselves to be really Christians still living for worldliness and frivolity, withholding the entire surrender of their whole being to the service of God ? See, dear friends, how solemn a thing it is to live, how Life connects you with God, and makes you so entirely His: and see that the life which you have so directly from Him, and which He so directly sustains, really manifests itself through you as *His* life, and not yours. Spend it in doing His will, and carrying out, to the utmost of your knowledge and power, the purposes for which He gave it you. Use it *as His*; and let it bring to Him the glory with which it is your privilege to glorify Him.

Bring the sad wasted life which is past to Him, whose alone it is. The blood of Jesus Christ, simply trusted by you, shall blot out the dark record against you; and now start afresh, accepted and forgiven, and let the future life be a daily and hourly recognition of the fact that your very life is His, and that it may be yielded up to Him most blessedly, in its every detail, and lived in such close union with Himself.

4

INFLUENCE AS TALENT

In considering influence as a talent to be used for God, we enter upon a very important branch of our subject. That influence is a talent, and that each must look upon it as 'My Lord's Money,' none would, of course, deny; yet few have practically accepted this truth in all its bearings.

The subject is a wide one, because it includes so large a portion of the entire life. Almost every question connected with each detail of outward daily life comes, in one way or another, before the Christian as a matter of influence on others about him. In a very real sense, it touches the very root of a consecrated life.

The first point to settle is to recognize that all influence is a trust *from* God. To accept this in theory is easy enough; but to enter into it as a reality is what we mean. The temptation arises when a position of influence has been gained, to regard it as the result of a natural energy of character, which has made its impression upon others.

Nehemiah, on the other hand, after gaining a remarkable

influence over the Eastern monarch in whose court he lived, and then over his own people on his return to Jerusalem, instead of ascribing it to his own remarkable energy of character, so often speaks of it as due to 'the good hand of his God upon him' (Nehemiah 2:8). He recognized so fully that it was *from God*. To remember this is the great safeguard in every position of influence we may reach. The very energy of character by which we have reached it is itself a talent entrusted to us. And the influence gained by it is but the result of trading with it to the best advantage.

And here we may say a word on the responsibility of so laying out our talents, not only as to obtain a full reward when the Master reckons with His servants, but also as to increase and intensify the talents themselves, so that they may operate in a wider sphere . This will apply in various ways to everything that can properly be called a talent. But as regards the special subject before us now, we would urge the duty, as well as the privilege, not only of using influence that seems just thrown in our way, but of definitely seeking influence wherever it may be found. And those who seek it will find it literally on every side.

But there is amongst real Christians a great deal of energy of character which might be turned to so much account in the cause of Christ, but which simply runs to waste, so far as spiritual results are concerned. Few people, perhaps none, are utterly devoid of some energy in one direction or another. Others have a considerable amount, which they expend in their businesses, their domestic occupations, and in a variety of ways which fall in with their inclinations and tastes. But so few consecrate this to the service of God, and use their highest energies in seeking influence which they can exert for Him. How many Christians take the lead in business, in the household, in the school room, in the amusements, and, alas! sometimes in folly and vanity, who take no lead in the interests of Christ and His kingdom. We oftentimes long to see active, energetic people; who can influence others and take the lead in almost anything else, spend their energy for Christ, and take a leading part for Him. The truth is, that too many Christians do not live so closely to God as to see the reality of spiritual things; and so they lose sight of the unspeakable blessedness of definitely *seeking* influence of a spiritual sort.

These thoughts will come home in various ways to all; and to none more than to those who may be thinking that they have 'so little influence.' Not that we believe this to be really the case with anyone. People think so because they have not fully realized what influence they really have. But we say to those who complain of having so little, that the fault is probably in themselves. Have they sought it? Have they well laid out the little they believe themselves to have? Has a holy determination to exert an increasing influence for Christ really been formed by them? Let each of us judge ourselves here; and we shall probably find that we all might exert much more extensive influence than we do. And many most likely will find that they are, to a large extent, hiding their Lord's money, like the slothful servant in the parable.

But there is danger in the very use of our talents. The original talent multiplies itself; and as it grows by exercise, it opens before us new positions of special influence. It becomes, so to speak, a talent of a higher order. And as we become conscious of its possession, we must carefully avoid the danger already pointed out, of looking upon it as the produce of our own energy, instead of only as the further bestowment of trust from our Lord Himself, or as Nehemiah expresses it, 'the good hand of our God.'

Or again, if in spite, as it were, of ourselves, and through no special effort on our part, but merely, as we should say, through 'force of circumstances', such as birth, marriage, inheritance of means, selection by others, we find ourselves in positions of special influence, we are not free from the danger already mentioned. We are so apt to refer it all rather to circumstances, than to trace it up directly to the hand of God, as a talent from Him, and to be used for Him. Of course, in a general sort of way, as Christians, we believe the circumstances to be indications of the will of God concerning us. But all power from the thought is to many lost just by 'the general sort of way' in which it is entertained.

If our influence, however, is to be rightly used and increasingly exerted, the first great secret is really to recognize that, be it apparently great or little to begin with, it is distinctly *from God*. This is equally true whether it seems to spring from any natural energy of character with which He has endued us, and which, properly used, must increase our sphere of influence; or whether it comes to us almost in spite of ourselves, by the force of circumstances. And it will help us to recognize this when we realize that our natural endowments of character, as well as the outward circumstances which determine our various spheres of influence, are every one of them God's *personal and individual dealings with each of us*. They are measured out by Him, proportioned to each of us as seems best in His sight. He knows the use for which He needs each one of His people; and He supplies the points of character, or the surrounding circumstances, in which each can best do Him service.

This brings us again, as we said in regard to the possession of life itself, into very close contact with God, giving us each, in so special a manner, our own individuality before Him, both as to our endowments for usefulness in His service, as well as to our responsibility in using them. And while it makes us thoroughly contented with the state of life in which it has pleased Him to call us, it also supplies the right motive for the direction and control of that desire 'to rise in life' which is instinctive in us all.

But we must not forget the human side of it. God gives us the endowments of character and of outward circumstances *for use*. And we are by diligent use of them to extend them further. We should endeavor so to exercise all the energy of our character, and so to improve our outward surroundings, that we may obtain a wider sphere of usefulness in which to exercise an influence for Him.

With this motive definitely in view, the Christian may make every use of all his sanctified energies and his consecrated earthly circumstances to advance in life, and to reach the highest attainable position, in order that in it he may the more widely extend the interests of the kingdom of Christ. Here is the great aim of really sanctified ambition. And let every Christian, while earnestly avoiding unworthy and doubtful methods of advancement, yet lose no right and proper opportunity of 'getting on in the world,' if his new and extended sphere is but a wider platform upon which to make known to others 'the unsearchable riches of Christ.'

But it is also most important to bear in mind that influence is not only a talent entrusted in a general way to each one of us; but also that, in a most real sense, it is one which is constantly passing out of our hands beyond recall.

This is, of course, solemnly true of each opportunity, trifling as it may be, of exerting influence for God in the various circumstances of life, from hour to hour. These opportunities are constantly coming and going. They present to us some opening for advancing the kingdom of Christ which, humanly speaking, may never be again within our reach. The particular person with whom we have been thrown in contact, and who might have been spiritually influenced by us; the opening which some one otherwise almost unapproachable, gave us of saying a word for Christ, or of giving a suitable tract or book: the particular circumstance which might have been turned by us to good account; the particular conversation which might have been led up by us to something spiritual; the opportunity for exhibiting a Christian spirit under a passing provocation or disappointment; the occasion for witnessing for Christ, in a loving and winning way, against some worldly conformity as to dress, as to habits of society, as to amusements, and such like; all these, and numberless similar openings for Christian influence, quietly pass by, and too often, when once let slip, are beyond our reach for ever.

This is one aspect of what we mean by saying that influence is a talent which, in one sense, is constantly. passing out of our hands. And it requires not only a real and abiding sense of our responsibility as to such matters, but also much constant watchfulness as well as much waiting upon God for guidance, in order that we may, in the first place, recognize these openings for influence as they occur, and then make the very best use of them while they last.

But there is also another most important aspect of our present subject. Over and above these constantly recurring openings for exercising influence which every condition of age and circumstance holds out, there are those special openings which each *period of life* brings with it, and which, with each period of life, is passing away.

There is the influence special to childhood. Of course, we know that persons of all ages may influence children; but children themselves have an influence among children which no grown person can exercise. They can exhibit amongst the special difficulties of child-life the temper and spirit of Christ; and show their little brothers and sisters, relations and friends, what it is to be a really Christian child. And then from the children's standpoint, and in their own simple language, they can speak the childlike word for Christ which can awaken an echo in other young hearts. It would be well for parents, elder brothers and sisters, teachers at church, and all who are connected with children, to teach them the privilege of exercising an influence for Christ, which none but themselves can exert.

But this passes away, and then comes the period of school-life. In whatever rank of life young Christians move, and be they boys or girls, it is precisely the same. Great beyond description is the influence in a school of one decided young Christian, who really lives the Christian life, and shows how it supplies a power to resist all the varied temptations of school-life, and how it affords a peace and joy to which others are strangers. Such an one has an influence which no head of a school, however much in earnest, and no governess or teacher, can exercise. But it is special to school-days. And it is quickly passing away.

Moreover, it is passing away not only in the sense that school-days themselves are passing by, and will in time be over; but more specially so, because those who may be influenced by young Christians at school, as by no one else, are constantly coming and going. Each term at every school brings its changes. Some new ones come often from worldly homes, where religion was almost unknown; others leave to meet the temptations of the world; and the time for exerting an influence for Christ over them all is too precious to lose. Very many, we can well imagine, who have been brought to a sense of their responsibility before God in the matter of influence later in life, are deeply sensible of having lost the grand opportunities afforded by school-life.

Then, when school-days are over, there is the special influence, which no one else can so powerfully use, of the young men or the young women amongst their equals in age and condition of life. This period of life is beset with its peculiar and powerful temptations; and the exhibition of a bright, happy Christian life, and the winning words quietly spoken for Christ, by those who are passing through the same temptations, have a power which no 'advice' from their elders can have, however kindly it may be given. The young man can influence the young man, the young woman can influence the young woman, both by word of mouth and by example of life, as those more advanced in life can never do. The elder ones at all events are supposed to have 'sown their wild oats' in youth, and now to have 'sobered down' as age advanced. And this idea too often detracts much from the testimony of their elders in the eyes of young men and women. But here is the real power of Christian young men and women. Here is a talent, which is entrusted to them for a while; and it must in time pass away.

But then, as middle life opens out, it brings its own special opportunities of usefulness. The cares of business and family life afford openings for Christian influence, which can the most powerfully be used by those in a similar position. Otherwise, the kind and well-meant exhortation is regarded only as *theory;* and the testimony is weakened by the thought that the Christians who seek to exert an influence for Christ would not be so bright and happy were they similarly beset with cares and anxieties. But here is a talent of influence for those who are surrounded by the sterner realities of life. They can speak for Christ with a power which is peculiar to themselves. They can *show*, as none else can, by an earnest active Christian life, that it is possible to do the business of this life heartily and well, and yet amidst it all to 'seek first the kingdom of God and His righteousness.' But this in its turn is passing away.

And then there is the peculiar influence of old age for those who are spared to reach it—the special testimony which only those can bear with power who have passed through the previous experiences of life, and are able to influence in a very special way the aged around them.

Of course, we do not by any means *limit* the Christian's sphere of influence to his special condition of life at the time being, but we mean that these special conditions of life afford the most precious opportunities, and all the more precious because they quickly pass away.

We feel that this part of our subject has only been very briefly opened out; but sufficient has been said to suggest careful thought, Let all our readers consider whether they are 'occupying' the special spheres of influence which their age and condition of life are for the time holding out.

Our consideration, however, of influence as a talent to be laid out to the glory of God, would not be complete without some remarks on what may be called *unconscious influence*. It may seem to some that 'unconscious influence' involves almost a direct contradiction in terms. The moment we think about how to use it for the Master, it ceases to be, strictly speaking, 'unconscious.'

No doubt there is a certain amount of truth about this. But at the same time it is undeniably true that there is a general sort of influence to be used for God, which almost every hour of the day calls into action in an unspeakable variety of ways. These opportunities so suddenly come, and as suddenly depart, that they are scarcely recognized at all, even by those who keep the most careful watch for any openings which present themselves for exerting an influence for God.

Sometimes, and possibly very often, they are wholly unobserved by us. But it is an unspeakably solemn fact, that we are thus continually making impressions, either for good or evil, on those with whom we are daily and hourly associated in the various relationships of life; impressions which often remain fixed upon their minds for many a long year. But yet still more solemn is the thought that the spiritual destiny of some, the question, that is, as to whether they are saved or lost, as well as the spiritual growth of those who are really converted to God, may often, humanly speaking, turn upon the sort of influence which we may exercise over them in ways of which we are perfectly unconscious at the time.

That the believer in Christ, who makes a decided and open profession of faith in Him, is watched by the world, by mere professors of religion, and even by his fellow Christians, is only too true. They expect something higher and better from them, and very naturally. But it is not of this which we speak now. The unconscious influence to which we allude, is that which we exercise over others without their specially watching us. It is not so much the result of the open lines of action which we take up, after careful consideration as to what it is right to do, and which we know will be weighed and discussed by others. It is rather the result of 'just the manner displayed, the tone adopted, the smile, the frown, the silence, or the remark dropped; the calmness, or the reverse, under provocation or worry; the choices which we make in little things; the turn which we give to a passing conversation; the exhibition of self-sacrifice, or self-seeking, in little trivial matters; the books we are seen to enjoy; our lesser personal habits; our methods of personal attire and dress; and an almost endless number of similar things.'

To lay down any rules for the employment of unconscious influence would be obviously impossible. The only suggestion that we can make with regard to it is, that we should endeavor to maintain the general spiritual tone always high. We should endeavor to keep the consciousness of our own salvation bright and clear, and to exhibit always the happiness and joy which become a Christian. We should seek to live in the light of God's presence, and to cultivate the habit of bringing the smallest details into it. It is only as we do so that we shall grow into what we may call the unconscious habit of using this special sort of influence on the Lord's side.

5

SOCIAL POSITION

It is most important that those who desire their talents to be wholly consecrated to God should not overlook their *social position*, as being distinctly a portion of their 'Lord's Money,' which may and should be turned to the very best account.

In a general way everyone would agree to this; but it is just 'the general way' in which people assent to a truth that robs it of its practical force. To be practically applied, a truth must be very definitely accepted. This we desire to bring about in regard to the social position of each one of our readers.

By 'social position' we do not mean only the higher and more prominent stations in life, which belong to very few. Some think that they have little or no social position at all, because they are not in the front ranks of society. But in reality *all* have their social position, whatever be their rank in life; for by social position we mean that particular place in society, higher or lower, which each one is called, in God's providence, to fill.

What we have said already as to the power of influence, exercised in each period of life over our equals in age, is also true as to our various positions in life. Our most powerful sphere of influence ought to be over those in a similar social position to ourselves.

This, however, is where most people signally fail. Even those who, from their engaging in some distinct sphere of Christian work, are called 'Christian workers,' for the most part direct their main efforts at a class of life socially below them. Sometimes, no doubt, circumstances render this advisable. Indeed, it is one way in which a higher social position may sometimes be *still further* consecrated to the Lord, when in the church service, by a Bible class, a mother's meeting, a district or hospital to visit, or in any other way, influence is used for God over those in a lower social rank.

But for all this class of work a higher social standing is not in itself an absolute *necessity*, however much in some cases it may be advisable. Outspoken, decided profession, a really consistent life, and a careful study of the Scriptures, will gain for one in almost any social position an authority for such work amongst those who are socially their equals. And very often it is a positive advantage when such work can be done by persons in much the same rank of life as those whom it is sought to help.

Anyhow, it is not from Christian work done amongst those lower in the social scale that one ought to deserve the title of 'Christian worker,' but rather from the fact that one is engaged in exerting all possible influence for God amongst those in one's own class of life. Indeed, one chief objection to Christian work being carried on amongst those in a lower social position is, that such workers too often settle down contentedly in it, and confine themselves entirely to it.

They consider themselves 'Christian workers' because of it, when in reality they are overlooking the *real* work which God has placed before them in their own social sphere, and so are 'hiding in the earth' their *real* talent. They have *chosen* what they think to be *their work for God*, instead of just *taking up* what is *God's work for them*, which lies in their own social circle.

The true 'Christian worker' is the one who seeks to influence souls for God in his own social sphere first of all, and with whom all out side work (commonly known as 'Christian work') is over and above this, instead of *in place of it.*

How it would exalt and ennoble even the most ordinary and humble life, and what a grand and yet solemn object for which to live would at once appear, if we were each to recognize that our individual social positions are really talents committed to our trust for the advancement of the kingdom of God *in that particular sphere,* and that our Lord will hereafter 'reckon' with each of us as to the use we have made of it for Him.

No doubt, it is much easier to exert influence for God amongst a class socially lower than ourselves. A higher social position in itself gives a sort of standing and authority, and makes the way comparatively easy, although some do little or nothing even from this standpoint of advantage. Moreover, those in a lower rank of life are not in a position to observe the blemishes in the character which so much weaken or discredit the religious influence of so many amongst their equals in life. They do not see the worldly conformities, the frivolous spirit, the hasty temper, the unkind judgments, the bitter words, and similar personal failings, which are evident enough to those socially equal.

The fact is, that an altogether higher attainment in personal holiness of life is needed for Christian work amongst our equals. For this, one must be very *real*; and here, no doubt, is the reason why so many let such work alone. There are many 'Christian workers' who have earnestly spoken for Christ in some outside sphere, and possibly even to their servants, but who never do so to their own family, to relations and personal friends. To these their lips are sealed, because of more or less frequent failures in evidencing that truly Christian spirit which must be manifested in those who would work for God amongst their own relations and friends.

Sometimes, in those who do much outside work, and who for consistency of conduct *might* be witnesses for God amongst their own equals, there is a strange shyness which hinders them from exerting the influence which they might. This is a sinful weakness; and the only remedy is in a more direct and implicit faith that God can and will supply the requisite confidence at the right moment, and also give success to the effort.

To all our readers, then, whatever be their position in life, we would say, 'Earnestly qualify yourselves, by a decided religious profession, and by a life which all will recognize as being really answerable to it, for what is your first and special sphere of Christian work; and, thus qualified, seek every opportunity of exerting an influence for God amongst those who are your equals in life.'

But what can they do? This must be left very much to the judgment of each one. We shall, however, suggest a few practical thoughts, which we hope will be generally useful.

By those socially equal with ourselves, we must first of all, in whatever rank of life our lot is cast, understand the members of our own families, our children, our parents, our brothers, our sisters, or any others who live with us, as the case may be. Those who are bound to us by any ties of relationship should next claim our attention. Then comes the circle of our friends and acquaintances; those also with whom we may be thrown, whether in the office, the place of business, the workshop, the factory, the school, or wherever the scene of our daily occupation lies. In all these spheres of work, the methods to be used for exerting an influence for God are very much the same.

First, of course, there are the words which may be spoken for God. We may speak to others kindly and lovingly, either by way of convincing of sin the worldly and careless, or of helping the seeking ones, or of comforting the sorrowful, or of building up and encouraging in their Christian course those who need it.

There is not as much of this as there ought to be. We have known cases in which even the professing Christians of a family never speak to each other about Christ. This is a sad state of things. But there is very special need for Christians to speak on the subject of vital religion to those who make no such profession.

This is not nearly so difficult as some would think. Very often the ice has only to be broken, and the worker finds, even under what appears a worldly and thoughtless exterior, a longing for something better, a real pleasure in being spoken to about the things of God, and sometimes even deep anxiety of soul. Or, as the result of speaking, the worker often discovers in another a weak and faltering Christian, who would never have had courage to *begin* such conversation, but who may be much helped and strengthened by Christian intercourse, and will afterwards not shrink from commencing to speak.

Only, in all speaking for God, let the following suggestions be carefully observed:—

SUGGESTION #1: Aim at speaking about *real, vital religion*, about Christ as a personal Savior from sin and sorrow. Many satisfy themselves with very vague and vapid 'religious talk' on generalities, which does little good. Seek to be personal, and to bring home the realities of religion to the heart and conscience. Show people that you want to lead them not to mere formal religion, but to vital godliness.

SUGGESTION #2: Speak as little as possible of *yourself*. Be ready to bear your quiet testimony, that you find in Christ, and in following Him, all your soul-needs satisfied. But let that suffice. Some well-meaning Christians leave the impression that they have said much more about themselves than about Christ. What *He is*, and, if you like, what *you find Him*, but not what *you are*, must be your theme.

SUGGESTION #3: Avoid that assumption of spiritual superiority which makes the testimony of some Christians so objectionable to the careless and worldly. Be careful not even to appear to be scolding them. Remember that it is only through free and unmerited grace if you are any better than others. Stand on the same level with them. Let them feel that you have sympathy with them. Seek to *lead* them higher, and not to *drag* them. Speak tenderly, kindly, winningly, lovingly, and you will find a way to many hearts.

SUGGESTION #4: Speak at *suitable* times. Any time will not do. Much harm is often done by speaking to people before others. They naturally resent it. Get people quietly, alone, and, if possible, when they will not be hurried. Avoid speaking when they are ruffled in temper or agitated by circumstances. Watch your time. Nothing so much needs a sanctified judgment, aided by earnest prayer for the promised wisdom (James 1:5-6).

SUGGESTION #5: *Lead up to your subject.* Many do harm by abruptly asking a pointed question. It takes people aback, and often gives them a sort of shock which only hardens them against religion. Try rather to lead up a conversation to the main point. A spiritual mind can give a spiritual turn to almost any conversation, no matter what is the subject in hand. A conversation commenced about a sermon or a religious book will easily take the needed turn. But any subject can be used for the Lord.

SUGGESTION #6: Do not be *always* talking at people. Let them feel that they can be with you, even alone, without being always 'attacked.' Try and win people's confidence by entering cheerfully into subjects which interest them, and by joining, so far as you can innocently do so, in their pursuits and recreations. Let them see that to be really religious does not mean to be morose and dull.

But speaking is not the only way of exerting an influence for God amongst our equals in life. Or a favorable opportunity for speaking may never arise. What else can be done?

There is the *presentation of a book*. This, when it can be afforded, is better than a tract, to which many people strongly object, and which some even receive as almost a personal insult; as if they were considered specially wicked. A birthday, Christmas, the New Year, or any other *special* occasion, affords an opportunity for giving a helpful book of a spiritual sort, without the appearance of any meditated design, which some so sensitively resent. There are some, of course, to whom such a book may be given at *any* time; but it is not so with every one. Some require more careful treatment.

But it is so needful to select a book which is really suitable. Some Christians have very little discrimination. As long as a book is 'religious,' they think that it will suit anyone. But there are books suitable for awakening the careless; others for helping the anxious; and others for leading on the believer; and the spiritual condition of those whom we wish to help should, as far as possible, be considered in the selection of a book, as carefully as the physician thinks of the case of his patient in the choice of a remedy.

Thus to gain an acquaintance with the contents of religious books, with a view to their judicious use, should be the aim of the true Christian worker. And to purchase them for such use is a very important method of employing one's money, much or little, as a talent in the Master's service.

Exactly the same may be said of tracts, when books cannot be afforded. Much of the objection to the receiving of tracts arises from their *injudicious* distribution. Some startling title, meant to be 'striking,' is liable to be considered offensive; or there is a harsh denunciation of sin, instead of loving exhortation to the sinner; or the truth is obscurely put. To write a good tract requires much care; but just as much is needed in the selection of one to give away, if we really wish to 'hit the right nail on the head.' Let Christian workers collect tracts, and read them, and then lay in supplies only of what they think will be useful. Prayer for guidance should accompany the selection in each case, and prayer for blessing the delivery.

Then, we may seek to influence for God our equals in life by lending or recommending them good and helpful books to read; by bringing useful periodicals to their notice, encouraging them to subscribe; or by inviting them to go with us to religious services where we think they may receive a blessing. In a very special way we may do so by persuading them to join some Scripture Reading Union.[1]

Then, again, there are the absent ones. To these we may post the book or the tract. But letter-writing, by which we can earnestly and lovingly plead with them, or else seek to remove their doubts and difficulties, is a talent which we may lay out so as to secure a large spiritual return. Christian workers should encourage their friends to write to them on spiritual subjects. Some people will do so more readily than they will talk about them. And many Christians can write what may be helpful more easily than they can say it.[2]

Another method of influencing those who are socially our equals

---

1. For a notice of the Christian Progress Scripture Reading Union, see at the end of this volume.
2. The subject of writing letters for God is fully dealt with in a chapter further on, entitled "The Consecrated Pen."

is to arrange (where it is possible) 'drawing-room meetings,' either in our own or in some one else's house, for Bible readings, addresses, or on behalf of various religious works. Many will attend such as these, who would never go near an ordinary religious meeting.

Where these are not possible, smaller meetings for Bible reading and prayer, if only very few can be got together, are of great use. This can be done in the humblest cottage just as well as in the largest house. It is a method open to all classes of life. Many young people could gather together a few of their young friends in this way, and usefully influence them. A Bible class for the children of those in the same position of life as oneself is always a useful thing, and often much appreciated by parents who would allow their children no other sort of distinct religious teaching.

We have now suggested several ways in which as real 'Christian workers' we may seek to make use of our 'social position' as our 'Lord's Money,' by exerting influence for God over those in our own station in life, whatever that may be. But, of course, this does not exhaust the responsibility in very many cases. When our social position is such as to give us a special influence over others socially below us, we must make the most profit as well. Employers of labor (whether it be of many or few 'hands' employed in manufacture, or of the small staff of servants in their households), heads of schools, persons in any sort of command or superintendence, will do well to recognize their social position as their 'Lord's Money,' entrusted to them for use in the particular direction in which their influence lies.

Those, too, in the humblest positions in life will find in them their sphere of usefulness. Much that has been suggested above will apply, in its measure, to these also. Their power for usefulness lies specially amongst their equals in life. The poorest cottager will find that efforts such as we have described to exert influence for God, backed up by simple, unaffected piety, will go further and accomplish far more real work in cottage homes around, than all the visits of the squire's family or the district ladies, useful as these may be.

Then, too, let it be remembered that our social position, whatever it is, brings us within reach of work which those in other positions, higher or lower, cannot do. The operative in the workshop, or the assistant in a large house of business, has, by personal contact and daily intercourse, an opportunity for influencing his fellows which the head of the firm can never have. The boy or girl at school, for the same reason, has an opening for influence which the master or mistress cannot reach. The young man in the parish or congregation can bring an influence to bear on the young men around him which the minister can never exert.

The same thought will apply to almost every position that could be named. Each has its own sphere of influence which is special to it, and all should see that they are 'putting their Lord's Money to the exchangers,' that 'at His coming He may receive His own with usury' (Matthew 25:27).

6

EDUCATIONAL ADVANTAGES

Much that we shall say in the present chapter will refer to our younger readers who are passing through the period of school life. But we shall also try to suggest ways in which those who are beyond this may still make the best use of the talent under consideration.

During their younger days, when it is just the time to make the most of them, we fear that very few take the highest and the only right view of their educational advantages. It is too commonly when school life is over, and the best chances for laying in stores of useful learning have passed away, that people wake up to see how different it might have been, had they in earlier days learned to consecrate their studies to the service of God.

That educational advantages are among the talents entrusted to us, and should therefore be regarded as our 'Lord's Money' received from Him to be laid out in His service and to promote His kingdom and glory, can admit of no doubt. These should be made the subject of as definite consecration to God as any other more recognized talent. And the earlier in life this is done, the greater is the happiness and the wider usefulness which result.

What a difference it would make in school days, if all the lessons were viewed as opportunities of serving God, not only for the present moment, but also in view of accomplishing in the future His will and work! The drudgery which some find in school studies would be removed; and a pleasure and interest would be added, over and above the delight which some young people take in acquiring knowledge, if exercises were done, lessons were learnt, music and drawing were practiced, all *for Christ.* And yet such a life is really open to every boy or girl at school who has first accepted Christ as a personal Savior, and has, by simple consecration of self to Him, become His disciple.

When once this principle has been grasped in reality and acted upon, then all the reasons for making the most of educational advantages (even those which might seem, at first sight, to savor of merely worldly motives) are raised into the sphere of religion, and appear as service done to God for Christ's sake.

Such a motive sanctifies every other, which without it might seem of a more selfish sort. Nothing is really selfish which has Christ for its absorbing object, however much one's own interests may also be wrapped up in it. The interests of Christ and of the true believer in Him are so thoroughly one, that they cannot be considered apart. So far as the believer has learned to regard all his advantages in life as his 'Lord's Money' entrusted to him, and to use them all in the service of Christ, so far all this becomes a reality.

There are several reasons for making the utmost use of educational advantages, all of which, in one way or another, may be regarded as service for God, and as the laying out of His 'Money.'

There is the duty which young people owe to their parents, to honor whom, according to God's commandment, is to honor God Himself. Parents spend money on their children's education, and in many cases it can ill be spared. Anyhow, it is an investment or outlay of money, the only interest or return on which is what the parents receive as the results of their children's studies. They can repay their parents by that diligence and steady work which always, even with those who are not 'clever,' results in progress and proficiency. A well-educated son or daughter, after leaving school, adds much to the brightness and the general welfare of the home circle. Proficiency in languages, literature, art, or science can always be made to give pleasure to parents in a variety of ways, and also can always find topics of interest to attract or amuse brothers, sisters, and friends.

Moreover, children who have made the most of their own education can often repay their parents by teaching the younger ones at home; or they can help their parents by earning something as teachers, should the need arise; and the better they are educated, the more they will earn. Or they can do so by obtaining the higher and more honorable positions in life which are open to those who can pass a good examination.

Then, there is a duty which young students owe to themselves. Education is an advantage which spreads its influence over the whole after life. Over and above the considerations already named, which conduce so much to their own interests also as to those of their parents, is the fact that a well-educated mind is always a source of pleasure to oneself. It is full of interests, and can always find sources of agreeable and profitable occupation or amusement, and it can interest others in intelligent pursuits, and so give them higher objects in life than they would otherwise have. It can raise the general tone of thought and conversation around it. It can foster tastes in others which will tend much to remove the taste for frivolous and worldly occupations and amusements. We think that gatherings of young people for mutual improvement in various studies would in many cases displace those for doubtful recreations.

But we must now address ourselves specially to those who have left school, and who want to put the 'Money into the bank' (Luke 19:23) with which they have been entrusted, as regards education.

Our first advice is, that they seek, in every way such as we have suggested or which may suggest itself to them, to make their education a source of pleasure and profit to their parents and their home circle, and all for *the Lord's sake.* The picture drawn or painted with improved skill; the new piece of music mastered; the song prettily sung;[1] the information on a variety of subjects which a well-stored mind can give; the ability to converse or write in other languages during a trip abroad, or as occasion may arise—in these and countless other ways which will suggest themselves, educational advantages may in after life be made to give the pleasure of which we speak.

Then, should occasion arise for helping in the education of younger brothers and sisters, it should be entered into willingly and cheerfully, and not done reluctantly or dreamily as a mere matter of necessity. Parents should never be made to feel that it is a drudgery, undertaken, as it were, just to oblige them. Undertaken for the Lord, at the call of duty, which is only another way of saying, at *His* call, it becomes work for Him. It affords openings for testifying for Christ by patience, gentleness, and self-denial, manifested in the difficulties and trials which may arise.

Exactly the same may be said should circumstances point to earning money by teaching in other families. This also should be undertaken just as cheerfully at the Lord's call. It may be made an opportunity for much usefulness in the Lord's service.

Our next advice is, when school days are over, and so far as it is possible all through life, *keep up the studies,* and if they have been allowed to slip, catch them up as much as possible. This is where so many fail even who have made good use of school days. The labors of their early years are more or less lost, or, at all events, not improved and made use of as they might be. On leaving school they think that their 'education is completed,' and that they have done with it. One or two specially favorite things may be followed out; but that is about all, and not always even that. This is through forgetting that educational advantages are their 'Lord's Money,' to be laid out for Him.

We would further advise that all should definitely use all their educational advantages in *direct work* for the Lord.

In a general way, this may be done by the influence which

---

1. Music and singing arc more fully dealt with in the next chapter, on 'Musical Gifts.'

education gives. Every one has respect for a well-educated person. He is looked up to; he is often allowed to do or say what would be denied to another. And especially, he wins respect for religion in the world.

He removes the reproach (often too well founded) that piety and ignorance generally go together. He can bear witness for Christ in a way in which others cannot, and amongst people whom others could not influence. Education gives power; and when this power is consecrated to the Lord, and used for Him, it gives a standpoint of advantage for His work, which nothing else can do. Sanctified ignorance, no doubt, can do something for God; but sanctified knowledge will, in the present day, do more, and influence a far wider sphere.

But there are special ways in which educational advantages may be turned to the highest account in the furtherance of the Lord's work.

We have seen that they may be, as it were, turned into money for temporal uses, by teaching when needed. In the same way, where not needed for this, money may be earned for expenditure in promoting the kingdom of God. Many a good work could be helped in this way by those who have time on their hands.

Proficiency in almost any branch of study may be utilized in this and similar ways. Paintings, drawings, and texts sold have produced large sums for Christian work; or texts *well painted* are always an acceptable gift, and when hung up by the owners, perhaps merely as works of art, or even out of compliment to the giver, yet announce their silent message on the wall.

Then various openings through life may occur for the employment of languages, for which it is well to be in readiness.[2]

---

2. Titus 3:1: 'Ready to every good work,' prepared for it, that is, whether the actual opportunity should come or not. To be 'ready' is our part. The opening for the work comes at God's leading, in the circumstances of life. Let none think that because such openings are 'not likely' with themselves, there is no need for readiness. A consciousness of readiness will often quicken the observation to look for and notice opportunities, which would otherwise pass by unobserved.

Those who travel know well what this means. A knowledge of foreign languages enables them to select, for themselves or their friends, suitable tracts for distribution abroad, or to converse with, or to hold classes for, the neglected and ignorant souls which travelers always meet. Again, facility of translation into, or from, other languages may often be pressed into the service of God in one way or another. Occasionally special Christian work amongst foreigners in England opens out.

While on the subject of languages, we would strongly advise all who have left school either to keep up or to get up sufficient Greek to enable them to read the New Testament in the original language. It is by no means difficult to do. And a knowledge of foreign languages enables one to read other versions of the Scriptures, and thus to obtain often a fresh light on the meaning of a text.

Then, there are openings for teaching, and so ennobling the lives of poorer and less favored ones, in night schools, institutes, young men and women's associations, or by small classes in one's own house, whether in the country or in towns. Such teaching is always best done by those who have most thoroughly mastered the subjects they teach. Influence may thus be gained which may often be used for spiritual ends. Let none suppose that, unless they can teach a Bible class, there is nothing to be done for God; or even hesitate to impart to others what is called 'secular knowledge.' Direct work for souls will often spring out of such efforts as these; and this aim definitely in view will sanctify what might seem purely secular.

Then, those who are proficient in branches of study can often help their young friends who have not had the same advantages. The Students' Branch of *The Christian Women's Education Union* arranges correspondence classes for young ladies who wish for help in continuing their education. Competent teachers for these are always acceptable, and can do much good.

We have by no means exhausted this subject, but we have written enough to set all our readers thinking how they can best lay out their educational advantages, as their 'Lord's Money,' so as, directly or indirectly, to seek the extension of His kingdom.

7

MUSICAL GIFTS

By musical gifts we do not mean only those talents of a really high order which very few possess, but just such ordinary gifts of music as are bestowed, in greater or less degree, upon most people. We say, 'upon most people,' because some are certainly 'not musical.' Their gifts do not lie at all in that direction. They have no notion as to whether notes are in harmony or not, and to pitch correctly with the voice any note sounded on the piano is simply impossible, from the fact that they have 'no ear.'

We believe, however, that such people are comparatively rare; and certainly none should so class themselves until an opinion to that effect has been given them by someone really competent to do so. And even under such circumstances probably patience and practice will accomplish something. We think it the duty of all to be *as musical as they can*, and, however little the gift may be, to improve it to the utmost.

Some may never have definitely connected their music with religion, nor seen how each has its bearing on the other. But whatever may be really recognized as a gift of God has something sacred about it; and this is only another way of saying that all the conditions and circumstances of life are very solemn, and bring us into close relationship with God. All that He has given us is *for use* and not for *waste*, but for use only to His glory, and to do Him service.

But besides this general view of the matter, musical gifts can in so many ways be used to promote the glory of God, that their cultivation to the utmost extent becomes a very special duty as well as a very peculiar privilege.

We strongly advise all young people, at school and at home, to take advantage of every opportunity of learning and improving both in music and singing. They may at first find it a little irksome and difficult, and the practice or the lesson may involve the loss (as they think it, but not *really* the loss) of play-time; but in after years they will never repent it, nay, they will be deeply thankful even to those who '*forced*' them to learn.

The main aim, however, of this chapter is to suggest to those who have left school how they may best use what musical gifts they have, as their 'Lord's Money,' in His service.

We would first say, as we have said already of studies in general, that all should catch up what may have been lost since school days ended, and then not only *keep it up*, but strive to *improve it*. Let this thought be ever present, that the more proficient we are, the better we can serve the Lord with our talent. It is *His gift* to us to begin with; but there is a sense in which this, as well as every other of our endowments, is, in our improvement and use of it, *our gift to Him*.

Musical gifts may be *very directly* used to God's glory in a variety of ways.

First, as regards instrumental music. There is the organ, the harmonium, and the piano to be played at religious gatherings of different sorts. It is a great privilege thus to lead the singing at the worship of God, playing, in the highest possible sense, *to* Him and *for* Him. There are plenty of such openings, especially as far as the harmonium and the piano at lesser meetings are concerned. And it is well to remember that much of the spirit and life of a hymn depends upon the skill with which it is played.

Then as regards vocal music. There is the choir for the church, for the mission services, and other sacred purposes; and a really cultivated and nicely trained voice adds much to the beauty and power of the singing. And not in the choir only. It is a great mistake to place all the best voices in the choir. Some should be distributed about the church or the meeting, and these should sing out just as heartily as those in the choir. The singing wants leading *all over the building*, before all present will take it up. People who are not very musical want encouraging. They have not the courage to 'sing out,' if no one near them is doing so too. But a cultivated voice and a practiced singer anywhere in a religious service soon calls out much song to God from others around which might otherwise be hushed. Let those, then, who are prevented from taking a public lead in the choir, or are, perhaps, forbidden to do so by parents and others, take thus a private lead, to which none could rightly object, instead of fretting because they 'cannot sing in the choir!'

Then there is the power of solo singing. A hymn thus sung by *any* voice is not without effect under some circumstances; but a trained and practiced voice brings home the words to the heart with a touching force. Evangelists have found the power of this; and it is a power which all should cultivate. People who cannot preach can sing for God.

We do not, however, advise *young ladies* to come to the front in this way in larger public gatherings, unless the call of duty is very distinct and clear. But the mothers' meeting, the sewing class, the hospital ward, the factory room, or the sick bedside, afford openings almost everywhere. Many a toiling worker for daily bread, and many a weary sufferer, is soothed and comforted, and sometimes brought to salvation and peace, by gospel hymns touchingly sung to them. Young Christians who could not speak much for God could gather a few children or poor people together and sing to them 'the songs of Zion.' Some sorts of invalids might find here a quiet sphere of work. But there are wider and more general spheres m which musical gifts may be exercised to God's glory.

The home circle is one of the most important of all. Musical gifts add much to the happiness of home. They are a source of pleasure to the parents, who have laid out money for the teaching of them; and this should be well remembered by the children in after life. They should seek to repay their parents by making home bright and happy. Then, the sisters can do so much to keep a hold upon their brothers, and to keep them at home by music. There is a refining and elevating power about good music which may open the mind and heart to higher things, and perhaps to holy aspirations and longings, if suitable music is provided. Besides, after a hard day's work in business or professional life, music is a recreation well calculated to relieve the mental strain.

Then again, in *social gatherings* of friends, music is a useful resource. It gives pleasure to many. It takes the place of doubtful amusements, and, to a large extent, displaces unprofitable talk. And all this is *real work* for God. But to do it well, as the Christian should try to do everything he undertakes, requires practice and pains; and these are well laid out upon it, if the high end we speak of is really being sought. Time spent in quiet practicing, with this in view, may be regarded as spent for God.

Here arises a question which we have often been asked: Ought the Christian's singing to be confined entirely to strictly 'Sacred Music,' as it is called? We think, very decidedly, that it should not. Many have insisted strongly on such a restriction as the highest standard of consecration. But we think that the restriction results from an imperfect view of what consecration really is. It is not the music, any more than the conversation or the reading, being confined to what is only 'religious' (in the usual sense of this word) that constitutes a consecrated life; but rather all the duties and occupations which the general conditions of life require being so carried out with a view to God's glory, that they all become religious in (not the *usual*, but) the *real* meaning of the word, that is, part of our service to God. Otherwise, a really consecrated life becomes an impossibility to thousands of most earnest souls who are mixed up, almost to the full extent of their time, in the claims of business and family life.

No one would confine the conversation, the reading, or the drawing and sketching of a Christian absolutely and entirely to matters which would usually be called 'religious;' and if so, we hardly see on what grounds his use of music should be so restricted. All we would ask is, that he should seek to use his music, and everything else besides, either directly or indirectly to bring glory to God.

We believe that what some would call a 'secular' song becomes, in the most real sense, a 'religious' one, when it is sung with a definite view of promoting God's glory by doing good, either in a spiritual or temporal sense, to others. Again, what some would call a 'religious' song may become, in the most real sense, 'secular,' if sung with any motive of self-glory, such as display of voice, or from any *pride of being religious*, which (strange as it may seem) is a subtle and disguised form of temptation to many who, by natural character, rather *like* being different from others, and singular in what they do.

We have spoken of doing good to others 'in a temporal sense,' and this ought not to be overlooked. Many decided Christians seem to think that if they cannot bring people face to face with the realities of sin, and salvation in Christ, they do no good. But as we come to know more of what 'the mind of Christ' (1 Corinthians 2:16) means, we shall see that shedding *temporal* blessings of every sort on others is a Christ-like work. And among such temporal blessings is the effort to make their lives happy in every right and innocent way, and to afford elevating refreshment of mind after work, or to direct their thoughts to good and noble things (not in the ordinary sense 'religious'), in order to lead them still higher in time, as the way may open. Temporal blessings of as many kinds as possible should be showered freely on all whom we wish eventually to lead to Christ, if we would work in the Master's way.

Of course, we would place some limit on the 'secular' songs. Whatever is in the very least degree profane, or suggests doubtful thoughts and morbid or unhealthy sentiments, should certainly be avoided. But there are, without doubt, very many songs and glees, thoroughly healthy in tone, suggesting pure and noble ideas, to which no objection could be rightly raised by the Christian, and which may even be of the greatest use. They may not be what he would *choose*, if left quite to himself; but in family and social life he must consider the tastes and wishes of others in things which are not in themselves wrong.

It must be remembered that many who have not yielded their hearts to God (some, perhaps, in our own family circle) naturally do not care for sacred music, and it would not be wise to force it on them as the only alternative between that and nothing. A judicious yielding will gain an influence over such which can be used for God in a variety of ways.

Sanctified judgment must decide the matter in the case of each song. But when what is doubtful is proposed, the Christian should not shrink from kindly, but firmly and quietly, declining. At the same time, it would always be well at once to propose something better as a substitute.

We should not be prepared to say that every song at all amusing should be forbidden. All that is vulgar and tending to lower the taste and thought must decidedly be avoided; and this would probably include most of what are called 'comic songs.' But the possibility of being amused, in an innocent way, has certainly been implanted in us by God Himself, and no Christian could properly refuse to recognize and exercise it, within right and proper limits. We have sometimes wondered why some earnest Christians, who can innocently enjoy what is witty or amusing in conversation and reading, or in the relation of circumstances that have happened, should so rigidly refuse either to listen to or to sing a song which is amusing in the least degree. Little inconsistencies like this, which are quickly observed, do no good, and considerably weaken our testimony with others, when we have to raise our voice against something *really* doubtful or wrong.

But although, as our readers will see, we not only do not exclude 'secular' music, but give it a fairly wide sanction, we should equally object to excluding the 'religious.' Let there be both. The Christian who will sing a 'secular' song of a right sort will be listened to all the more readily, we believe, when he sings a 'sacred' one, and he should be careful to use whatever openings may occur in family or social gatherings for singing words which may reach the hearts of the hearers.

With regard to instrumental music, very few, we think, would contend for the absolute exclusion of all pieces not known as 'sacred.' For practicing purposes, they become a necessity, and we see no reason why they should not be played to others. But we should not shrink from declining, kindly, but firmly, to play music for dancing. The Christian should, to the utmost of his power, set his face against that.

One word about singing at concerts. We can see no reason why people should not meet in a more formal way than at friends' houses, to listen to music and singing, which is, after all, only what a concert really means. Musical talent is a gift from God, and may be exercised to give pleasure to others, within the limits, of course, of what a Christian can rightly play or sing, and when the glory of God, and not self glory, is the object in view. To Christian men we would draw no other limit than this to any public singing. But we do not think that public singing at concerts, and especially solo performing, is altogether consistent with that modest and retiring spirit which is one of the special adornments of true womanhood, and which seems so fast disappearing in our days. It is, however, a matter which we should prefer to leave to the sanctified judgment of Christian women, rather than lay down any hard and fast rule on the subject. It is one of those cases in which what might be well for one would be very inadvisable for another. It is best, however, to act always on the safer side.

8

THE CONSECRATED PEN

A consecration to God which is really wholehearted and without any conscious reserve, will most certainly include the use of the pen. This is a solemn responsibility, and is not so carefully fulfilled by many as it should be. The influence of letters on the minds and hearts of others, drawing the thoughts either towards God or towards the world, is a most important consideration. Few think of the mark which is made, even if only for the moment, upon other hearts and lives by a single letter. Letter-writing, then, is surely part of that 'Money' entrusted to us which may, by God's blessing, bring its return in our Lord's service, with its tenfold reward, when He inquires of us 'how much every man has gained by trading' (Luke 29:15).

The use of the pen as a means of promoting the glory of God is within every one's reach. To be able to write at all is the only qualification. It is always better to write well, for the sake of the reader; but it is not an essential to a 'consecrated pen.' The one who can hardly write a legible word may have as consecrated a pen as the most fluent scribe.

One aspect of the subject is, of course, a *negative* one, pointing to what a consecrated pen could not write, any more than a consecrated tongue could utter.

Real consecration to God makes a wonderful difference in this respect. Next to hasty words, there is perhaps no temptation more tempting to one who has a real or a fancied grievance than to write a sharp letter about it. To many it seems such a relief to a feeling of anger to give it vent upon paper. And if they did so, and then destroyed what was written, there might be less harm in it. But this would not satisfy the wounded feelings. The one who has injured us must *know* what we think of him, or we are not at rest. But a real consecration to God puts a stop to this. We can only then write what can be written *for Him*. When *His* honor is concerned, we may write strongly and decidedly; but when it is only a matter of expressing our own injured feelings, we shall stay the pen.

A consecrated pen will also be stayed about matters concerning others which it is unkind to repeat. At times we may be *obliged* to write unfavorably of others. The interests of truth and religion may require it. But let it only be done when we believe it to be *our duty to God* to do it ; and then let it be written very definitely *for Him*, very humbly, and very kindly.

Again, the very least bordering on the unholy or the profane, or the slightest jest about holy things, even in the most passing way, will have no place in the letters of the consecrated child of God.

Nor would a really consecrated believer write letters, especially to worldly friends, the whole tone and tendency of which is to paint the world, worldly amusements, worldly literature, worldly society, and all else that is 'of the world,' in an agreeable and attractive light. Our letters should never build up and encourage the worldly-minded in a life of worldliness. Christians are so apt to think that they must write of what will be interesting to their correspondents, and sometimes they lead even worldly people to wonder how they can, as professing Christians, write such frivolous and worldly letters.

We turn now to the *positive* side of the subject, to unfold what may be written by the consecrated pen.

In the first place, there are the openings afforded by the press. Many could write well for the Lord in this way, if they only knew it. We sometimes receive papers and verses of great promise and much use from young and hitherto inexperienced writers; and we think that every young Christian of any ability should try this service, if led to it by having something definite and special to say. The editor of a religious paper or magazine would quickly detect any real promise on the effort being submitted to him.

This, however, is not the gift of everyone; nor have all the opening set before them. It is well, then, to know that there are other ways in which the pen may be just as really consecrated to God's service without ever appearing in print.

We may do a great work for God among the souls of others by writing letters on the subject of religion. We may earnestly warn the careless and worldly. We may lovingly invite the anxious soul to Christ. We may strengthen and encourage the young or the trembling believer. We may give some fresh light and teaching to the growing saint. We may minister consolation in trouble, and soothe many an aching heart. We may cheer many a sickbed, and comfort many a departing soul.

But there are *special* advantages about writing letters for God in these or similar cases to which we shall now call attention.

ADVANTAGE #1: We can thus influence many who are beyond our personal reach. Through the post, distance is of little account. To another town, to another county, to another continent, we can send our written messages for God.

ADVANTAGE #2: Many can write who cannot speak well. They shrink from speaking. Some are young, and shy of speaking to any one, and especially to their elders. Some are nervously inclined, or from previous habits are unaccustomed to talking to others about their souls. We do not say that this *ought* to be so, and might not be overcome. But with many it *is* so; and writing is a way of meeting the difficulty, at all events for a time, and may eventually lead to openings for speaking, and to facility for it. Some, too, are not ready of thought and speech, and can so much better write what they want to say. They can think over it and pray over it, before they send it out on its errand for the Master; and so prepared, it will go with real power from Him.

ADVANTAGE #3: By writing we can often reach those who have no one else to help them. Some are quite alone in the world, or perhaps are surrounded only by frivolous and worldly relations and friends. They have none to speak to them of spiritual things. But the Christian whose pen is consecrated to God can often send a message for Christ to such as these, which would otherwise never be received.

ADVANTAGE #4: Writing is such a very *personal* method of dealing with souls, certainly not less so, and in some respects more so, than actual conversation. The letter is put into one's own very hand. It was written for that special person, and for him alone. He cannot help feeling this; and it comes with such peculiar force. For this reason, it is so much better for him than a tract just enclosed, useful as these often are. The tract was not written *for him*, but perhaps by an unknown hand, just for anybody; and it is difficult to realize *himself* as the one addressed in the printed paper. It is so different with a letter written *on purpose for him*. It is impossible to escape from the power of such individual and personal dealing without specially hardening himself to resist such a special appeal.

ADVANTAGE #5: A letter can be made so much more *suitable* than a tract, because it is written with a view to the special condition of our friends. Our knowledge of their thoughts and feelings guides us in the way we approach the subject, or the length to which we press it With some, we must go very gently and gradually to work. They would not bear too much at a time. A tract written for a general case often fails to meet the particular one; but a letter, prayerfully and thoughtfully written, with the special case in view, is far more suitable.

ADVANTAGE #6: Then a letter on the subject of religion forcibly suggests a response. A tract[1] just slipped into an ordinary letter when full of other things, suggests timidity in speaking about religion on our own part, and will not inspire confidence to do so in others. It leaves it to *them* to commence writing about their souls; and this they will be slow to do. It is easy for them to answer our letter and to omit all mention of the tract, or at the most just to thank us for it, without further remark. But a letter written to them on the subject, and perhaps about nothing else, cannot be so evaded, if it is answered at all. It opens the subject for the timid ones, and leaves them only the following it up. At all events, it does all that we can do in this way in leading others to Christ, or to a deeper understanding and enjoyment of Him.

ADVANTAGE #7: Letter-writing is also a very delicate and private method of reaching souls, and therefore so suitable and useful. The subject of the soul's condition before God is so sacred that it should be carefully and tenderly handled. We have little sympathy with those well-meaning but mistaken people who ask the most personal questions at any time and under all circumstances, sometimes in public and before others. They do often more harm than good. Many shrink from such dealing who are thankful for a quiet word in secret with a Christian friend. The more private the better; and no way is so private as a letter on the subject.

ADVANTAGE #8: Then a letter is the possession of a lifetime. A conversation, of course, may be blessed at the moment, and leave its impression on the whole life; or an expression, or even a single word, unheeded at the time, may remain in the mind, and bear precious fruit 'after many days.' But many details of a conversation are sure to fade from the best of memories. A letter, however, may be read over and over again, till every word sinks deeply into the heart. And even if neglected at the time, it remains as long as the letter is preserved, to be useful at some future time. The approach of

---

1. It is not that we would discourage the use of tracts and leaflets in letters. Far otherwise; we value them much. Let them be used freely. While they should never be a *substitute* for the special written word of exhortation, they may often be a *useful addition* to it. In business letters a tract enclosed may often do its work.

some dark hour, or perhaps a rising conviction of sin, will recall that letter, and it will be hunted up and read. It may often happen that months, and even years after they are written, and perhaps after the writers themselves have passed away, the letters of Christian friends may be a source of blessing and comfort to those to whom they were originally written, as well as to others into whose hands they may fall.

ADVANTAGE #9: Writing letters for Christ opens a sphere of work to so many who would otherwise do so little for the souls of others. There are thousands of Christians, young ladies perhaps especially, who have no pressing occupation, or who, at all events, have much leisure time, which they would gladly use for God. Very often their highest idea is to spend such time in fancy or other work in order to make a few shillings for Christian efforts. They are always ready to make things for 'Sales of Work;' and, no doubt, there are times in the day with all who live a family life when such occupation is very suitable, and turns to account hours which might otherwise be wasted. But directly spiritual work should, when possible, be preferred;[2] and here is such a work within their reach, and which may, even in the circle of a very ordinary acquaintance, be extended very widely, and be blessed very abundantly.

ADVANTAGE #10: Here, too, is an opening for the many who, from various reasons, are prohibited from active Christian work. Some are hindered by those in authority over them. Rightly or wrongly, they are forbidden to do any active Christian work; and they are tempted either persistently to resist, or to endeavor to break away from under control. Some seek to leave their homes, because they will not be so 'fettered.' But letter-writing for God will give ample scope to the most active minds and earnest hearts which will really accept *God's sphere of work for them*, which always lies within the conditions of life in which He has placed them, instead of seeking, outside these, *what they think is their sphere for Him*. Others, again, are prohibited from active Christian work by 'doctor's orders.' Their health will not admit of it. But their 'consecrated

---

2. See the remarks in the chapter on ' Time as a Talent.'

pen' will open out to them a sphere of work within their reach. Indeed, letter-writing is a sphere of work eminently suited for the delicate and invalids, and for all who, for constitutional reasons, are prevented from work which necessitates fatigue or exposure to weather. It involves little or no bodily strain. It is independent of rain or sunshine. It may be done from the couch, or even in pencil from the sickbed, whenever the mind is equal to the task. And probably no letter would have such weight as one written from the borders of the eternal world. None need lack a sphere of work who have consecrated their pen to God.

ADVANTAGE #11: Life and power could be thus thrown into so much aimless correspondence. There are some who are obliged to write many letters. It is 'expected' of them by a large circle of relations or friends; and any long silence is made a subject of complaint. No doubt it is right, as far as we can, to 'keep up' with relations and friends; but how pointless is so much of this letter-writing which *could* be turned to such real spiritual account![3] A thought might be handed on from the daily Bible reading,1 or a few notes from a sermon heard might be helpful to another, and so widen the preacher's sphere of usefulness. Thus the duties and civilities of relationship and friendship could be made the means of doing much work for God of a very useful sort, which perhaps we alone can do.

ADVANTAGE #12: Letter-writing is a method by which we may follow up work in those who have come under our influence at any time, or to whom we may have been a help, when they are removed from us. What would be otherwise a *temporary* influence may by this means be made *permanent*. The earnest pleading with a schoolfellow, the quiet influence exerted in early days over young companions, may be sustained through a lifetime by letters. Bible students who have passed through our hands, and are now gone out into life, may be still retained under our teaching in this way. Servants whom we

---

3. Hence the advantage of getting all our friends to join the same Scripture Reading Union (see the notice at the end of this volume), as they would be so much better able to appreciate a thought from the passages which they were actually reading at the time.

may have influenced for God, and have now left us—indeed, all who have at any time been the objects of our Christian work, can thus be kept in sight. Companions in business or in service, now parted from us, may thus be constantly made to feel our influence. Anxious souls whom we may have helped at any time to lay hold of gospel peace, or who have not yet laid hold of it, may be helped by us still.

But it is most important to see that our letter-writing is really a *consecrated* work. This means more than some might suppose. It is a long step beyond a merely general desire to do some good to others, carried out in a merely general way. About *real* consecration there is something very definite. It involves several ideas, all of which contribute to give special effect to our work, and to produce special results. In the matter now before us, of writing letters for God, true consecration will suggest, among others, the following considerations.

We must remember that the work is not *ours*, but *His*; not so much what we do for Him, as what He does by us. We are His instruments in the work which *He* is doing. This makes our position in the matter so solemn, and the work so real. It brings us into such close fellowship with God ourselves, that we find a personal blessing in it to our own souls, apart from anything else; for whatever increases, or makes more conscious to us, our own communion with God is an intense blessing to ourselves.

And this consciousness of fellowship with God in the work will exert its powerful influence in every detail of the work itself. It will call into deeper exercise the faith which produced it. Fellowship with God is, in the first instance, the result of faith; but the consciousness of this fellowship, in its turn, intensifies our faith. The two things act and react on each other. And faith, be it remembered,—that is, a very simple trust in God,—is the secret of real success in using the consecrated pen. It is essentially a faith-work.

We shall now trace some of the influences of simple faith on letter-writing for God.

In the first place, faith will see the necessity of directing its efforts, as far as it can trace them, in the channels of God's choice. It will seek to be 'led' in this as in everything else. It will not ask, 'To whom do *I like* to write?' But rather, 'To whom does *He* wish me to write?' Some people are so much more 'interesting' than others. Some seem so much more 'likely' to respond. It is a real pleasure to self to write to some; but not so much so to write to others. Some seem to appreciate our efforts; but some seem so cold. We shrink from writing to those who might take offence. And our choice to whom we shall write is very apt to be made from considerations of this sort. But consecration cuts at the very root of all this. It leads us to write just as readily to the most 'unlikely' and the most apathetic, as to the most 'promising' cases, if it appears to be the will of the Lord to do so.

And in trying to discover the line of God's choice, we should follow, as far as possible, the daily guidance of His providential leadings. Unless some one seems specially and forcibly, and yet unaccountably, laid on our hearts, we should select those who are in any way brought before us by each day's events. Let circumstances, viewed as from God, direct us. A letter received, or an old letter turned up, or a conversation in which anyone is brought to our remembrance, or some event naturally connected in our minds with a particular person, or the occurrence of a birthday[4] or other anniversary—these, and such things as these, if prayerfully watched, will often suggest those to whom we should write.

Next, as to what we shall write. Here, again, faith acts a prominent part. It is God's message which we have to send, not ours. It is what *He* would have us say, and not what we should like to say. The letter must be written, not only with prayer at its commencement, but in conscious fellowship with Him in every sentence. We must ask Him how to begin, and then how to go on. This is so necessary, because He knows exactly the case of the one to be addressed. Secrets unknown to us are all open to Him. The hand which holds our pen must be placed, as it were, in His hand, and He must guide it.

---

4. A *Birthday Book*, in which other events connected with our friends might also be inserted, as well as their birthdays, is a useful reminder for the exercise of a 'consecrated pen.'

This must be our principle with *each and every* letter, and not only our general intention, which we *take for granted* in the separate details.

We must see that in each case it really is so. When consecration takes a 'general' turn, it loses much of its reality; but its freshness and power is retained by definite exercise in all its details. In giving God's message, we should very clearly have this end in view. Every letter should have its *aim*. And this will appear increasingly important as the sphere of our correspondence increases. We cannot be always writing to everybody. To some we can write but very seldom; and this is all the more reason for making the deepest possible mark when we do write.

Then we must be as *direct* as possible, going right down to the root of the matter. Vague, indefinite allusions to religion will not do. They are more or less 'expected' in the letters of decidedly religious people, and are received and passed by as matters of course. Then there is a vapid and pointless style of religious writing which the world calls 'goody,' and to which it pays very little attention. Let us avoid it. Roundabout dealing, or 'beating about the bush,' should also, as far as possible, be avoided. A little of it may be necessary in some cases, just to make the way clear for the home-thrust; but this should be its only use. Salvation, either yet to be received or more deeply to be enjoyed, as the case may be, must be the one grand point. We have no time for lower aims. Careless ones want awakening and warning. Halting ones want to be led to decision. Doubting ones want doubts removed. Believers want fresh and deeper light. This leaves no room for mere pointless religious sentiment.

As to the language we use, we think that it should be, as much as possible, the very words of Scripture. God's own word is what we want to hand on, rather than our own reasoning. It is this which has such special promise of blessing (Isaiah 55:10-11). It carries with it far more weight than our words. We should try to weave it into the remarks which we make, and to adopt it as our own. We can thus send the message to others with so much more confident expectation of real results, than if it were only our own religious phraseology. For every quotation of Scripture language we should add chapter and verse.

But in the choice of language the mind should be unreservedly placed at God's disposal, and the very words sought directly from Him in definite faith that He will give the right ones for every case. There should be no feverish anxiety about that matter. The confidence that He gives the right words is also accompanied by the knowledge that He can bless any words. We sometimes imagine so much to depend upon our way of putting the subject, the force of our language, or the aptness of our illustrations, that we elaborate our sentences most carefully, and almost nervously, instead of just writing with the happy confidence that He gives us the language which He will bless, while we write in fellowship with Him.

Moreover, do not let us imagine that to be useful we must of necessity be lengthy. As our openings for usefulness increase, we shall find that we may have to write briefly to many. But this is no hindrance to a blessing. One text bearing on the case, with one brief pointed remark, may do as much good as page after page of our reasoning.

Then, we should endeavor to write with the utmost tenderness and sympathy. So much good is lost by neglect of this. Many very earnest Christians assume such a position of superiority, and write in such a supercilious spirit, that they offend rather than win others. *We must come down to the level of those whom we wish to help.* If it is those yet in sin, it must be as nothing but sinners saved by grace ourselves. Let us, like one greater than ourselves, take the sinner's place (1 Timothy 1:15). If it is halting and doubting ones, it must be as those who have once been very much the same. If it is a believer needing light, let us remember that this will ever be our own need also. If it is one 'overtaken in a fault,' it must be specially 'in the spirit of meekness,' conscious of our own liability to temptation (Galatians 6:1).

A word about 'results.' Every letter written in this spirit of entire consecration will, in the same spirit, be sent off with, and followed up by, believing prayer, and also with the most confident expectation that God will use it. There must be no wavering on this point. He may not use it just as we should like, or as speedily as we could wish, but He will surely make *His own* use of it; and this is all that true consecration can ever seek. If we are dissatisfied with *His* results, we are so far defective in our consecration. Real faith is assured that every effort of ours has its place in His dealings with those to whom we write, and will work out sooner or later His own counsels. Results are to be left in His hands. But results there must be. Only we should be careful not to imagine that 'results' can only mean an immediate success. Success may be long deferred; we may have to wait 'many days,' or we may never live to see it. There may, however, be more at work than we imagine. We cannot read the secret workings of the heart which we have sought to help; and the influence of our words may never be known to us. But influence of some sort they must have; and consecration to God leads us to rest satisfied that He knows exactly how far it has gone.

This thought will prevent our worrying over what appear to be 'mistakes.' Someone resents our well-intended kindness, or seems at all events colder to us than before; and we fear that we have done more harm than good in 'setting him against' religious impressions. We ask in perplexity, why it was that, acting, as we trusted, in full consecration to God, we were allowed to 'make such a mistake.' But we must not too speedily conclude that it was a mistake at all. It may have told far more than we imagine; and the very resentment or the coldness which we notice may possibly be the best evidence that our effort has really made its mark.

And further still, this consideration will prevent our giving anyone up as a hopeless case. There are no impossibilities with God; none are 'hopeless' with Him; and as real consecration looks only to Him, it sustains the energies which might otherwise become 'weary in well-doing.' Where we seem to produce no good effect, we shall renew our efforts, as the way seems open to do so, content to wait on still, and trusting God to do His own work by us in His own way, and at His own time.

9

MONEY AS A TALENT

No one, we think, would doubt for a moment that money is, in the fullest sense, a talent committed to our trust to be laid out by us as something belonging to God. But comparatively few have entered into the reality of the thought, and really regard every penny that they have as not their own, but *His*.

We will clear away, at the outset, two possible mistakes on the subject.

Many confine the idea of God's property to only a portion of their means, much or little, according as they are 'well off' or otherwise. Whatever they think that they ought to give in what they call 'charity' they look upon as God's share, as it were, of their income; and all the rest they regard as their own, and spend without any very definite reference to God.

On the other hand, we maintain that, not any portion only, be it great or small, of our income belongs to God, but absolutely the whole of it, without any deduction whatever. 'The silver is mine, and the gold is mine, saith the Lord of Hosts' (Haggai 2:8). This is often quoted by those who *want* money, as a reason for asking Him for it; but not so often by those who have money, as a reason why they should look upon every single penny of it as absolutely and entirely His. People mostly use the words to prove that money entrusted to *other people* belongs to God. But they do not so readily apply them to all that they have themselves; and very often not even to that which they regarded as belonging to God *before* it came into their hands, but which they seem to regard very much as their own, when once they get hold of it.

The view which we contend for was fully understood by David when, referring in his prayer to the offerings made for the Temple, he says, ' Of Thine own[1] have we given Thee' (1 Chronicles 29:14). What was given for the Temple was a special offering for a special work for Him, but all that remained, not given for the Temple, was equally His.

Now for the other mistake to be removed. This view of the matter brings all, without exception, within reach of our remarks. Some might suppose that a chapter on using money for God has not much to do with them. They have very little of 'this world's goods,' as people call them. They think that the rich have money for God, but that *they* have little or none. This mistake, however, arises from their having already adopted the former one, which we have just sought to remove. If they really looked upon all that they have as belonging, in the fullest sense, to God, they would see that they have money, however little it may be, to be spent for Him.

We shall return to this thought presently, but will first deal fully with the question of devoting a fixed proportion of our income to the service of God in such a way that it could be spoken of as 'given to Him.'

This is a subject of the very first importance. Until Christians awake to a deeper sense of what is not only their privilege, but also

---

1. Literally it is, '*From Thine hand* have we given to Thee,' meaning either that the gifts were taken out of His own hand, as it were, to give to Him, and were therefore so entirely His own before; or else, that they were so clearly recognized as received from Him, as to be His own still, even after their bestowment on the people.

their positive duty in this respect, they will fail to give to the Lord money which they ought so to give. And several serious evils will result.

> **EVIL #1:** They will themselves lose, at the Lord's coming, much of the 'reaping,' which in this matter is to be proportionate to the 'sowing' (2 Corinthians 9:6), when He rewards 'every man according to his works' (Matthew 16:27).
>
> **EVIL #2:** They literally hinder the work of the Lord. He is not, of course, dependent upon our money; but He graciously condescends to use it in carrying out His work. And, humanly speaking, work has often to be left undone for 'want of funds.'
>
> **EVIL #3:** Christian workers are driven to seek money from worldly and unconverted people by hard begging, or, worse still, by bazaars and similar doubtful expedients. If even Christians only understood how to give, all this would not be necessary. Large sums now spent otherwise would at once be available for God's service. Only they find it easier (hard even as it often is) to get money out of others than to give it themselves, and so they seek it in this way.

But we very earnestly invite attention to the following suggestions on this subject.

We have no mention in Scripture of bazaars, fancy fairs, concerts, etc., to raise funds for God's work. The only method there recognized is that of genuine, freewill gifts, the giver receiving no return for his money other than the promise of God's reward. Gifts like this, and not money squeezed and coaxed out of people who would not otherwise give, by the return of some fancied equivalent, is what the Lord delights to receive. But Christians know that cold-hearted professors are always ready to supply funds in return for excitement and pleasure, and so they fall back upon them, often actually professing to object to them, because they say that they cannot raise money without them. They abandon the God-honoring methods of faith and prayer, and encourage people in a principle as discreditable to a real Christian profession as it is dishonoring to God. We often doubt whether work which requires such methods is *really* God's work at all.

Under the old dispensation, God expected His people to devote a tithe or tenth part of their increase in a very special way to His service. It was observed as a religious privilege or duty long before the Law (Genesis 24:20, 28:22). It was embodied in the Law; and special blessing was promised to honoring the Lord with *the first-fruits of all increase* (Proverbs 3:9). The withholding of this was denounced as *robbing* God (Malachi 3:8-9). And in this latter passage God invites His people to 'prove' Him by 'bringing all the tithes into the storehouse,' and to see if He would not bless them abundantly.

Here, then, are two distinct and most important principles as to giving to God, which were not merely a temporary rule under the Law, but a custom from the earliest ages. A *definite portion was specially devoted to God's service*, the amount not being left to momentary inclination, but settled beforehand And *the gift was a first-fruits*, a first charge, that is, on all increase, and not settled by considering how far it could be spared.

We will now turn to the New Testament for its teaching about giving. It is to be in exact proportion to the income. 'As God hath prospered him' (1 Corinthians 26:2) is the rule. 'According to what a man hath' is the *measure* required, while 'a willing mind' is the *spirit* for giving (2 Corinthians 8:12). And thus we have what each one should 'purpose in his heart; not grudgingly or of necessity: for God loveth a cheerful giver' (2 Corinthians 9:6). Moreover, very definite promises are held out to the giver. He is said to *sow*, after which he is to 'reap,' either 'sparingly' or 'bountifully,' according to the sowing (2 Corinthians 9:6). Clearly, then, it is both the privilege and the positive duty of the Christian to carry out these scriptural principles in the disposal of his money. Let us briefly dwell on them.

PRINCIPLE #1: *There should be a definite amount devoted to God's special service.* The amount each must settle for himself; but it must be in proportion to his income. We think as a general rule that all should follow the Scripture principle and give a tenth. But many could devote far more than this. Five pounds so set apart from an income of £50 a year is evidently a far larger offering in the sight of God than a thousand pounds out of an income of £10,000. This appears from our Lord's remark upon the gift of the poor widow (Luke 21:3-4). The one would leave £45 to live upon; the other, £9000. And an old writer has well remarked that the real value of a gift is according to what is kept back, rather than the actual amount given. There are many who might give half their income, and yet be far richer than those who give their tenth.

Of course, there may be reasons why some who might be expected to give more must keep to the lesser proportion, such as larger necessary expenses, or the requisite provision for a large family, etc. But we say 'necessary expenses,' because this is a consideration which lies at the very root of the matter; and the Lord's people need very plain teaching about needless extravagance. It is a very common notion that one is perfectly justified in 'living up to one's income; ' and so long as people do not exceed this, they very lightly regard a large amount of extravagance which might easily be avoided. But our whole income is provided for us to use for the Lord, to live not 'up to it,' but *out of it,* and to see that any remainder is used in a way which He would sanction. The self-indulgence of wealthy Christians, who might largely give to the Lord what they lavish upon their expensive houses, their luxurious tables, their extravagant tastes, or their dress and other personal expenditure, is very sad to see. But the same spirit is seen also in poorer Christians in their smaller measure.

There are great advantages in having a definite proportion set aside for the Lord. The question of how muck to give is then a settled one. Most people would always have some little sum in hand for this purpose, and the only question would be how best to dispose of it to His glory. Giving would become a far greater pleasure than it often is; and certainly asking for money would be far more agreeable than it is, if Christians kept a sum set aside for giving away. Instead of complaining about 'so many calls,' they would be looking out for suitable cases to help, and be thankful to those who brought such to their notice.

PRINCIPLE #2: Then the proportion so set aside, whether large or small, should be a *first charge on our income*, it should be laid by before anything is used for other purposes; and our income available for our various expenses should be definitely reckoned as less by just this sum.

To many this would be easy. They have enough and to spare; and there is only needed the 'willing mind.' But some who have the 'willing mind,' or think that they have it, hold back from not quite seeing the principles involved in such a habit. They say at once that they would not see their way, with their various expenses, to adopt it.

In reference to this, we would make two remarks which may help some.

We would ask, in the first place, whether their expenses really are reduced as much as they might be. Is there not some needless luxury, or expensive habit, which might be laid aside?[2]

Then, there is a more important consideration still. This habit calls, perhaps more than any other, for *the exercise of faith*. We do not advocate giving away all the money in hand which the Lord has provided for meeting our needs, and 'trusting the Lord to pay the bills,' as some put it. But we do believe in a sober and systematic way of giving, regulated by sanctified common sense. And we think that when we follow out a principle so manifestly indicated by God's word, we may most implicitly trust Him to provide for us and ours. Those who *really* believe that all temporal blessings are at God's disposal can trust Him as regards future supplies, so far as never even to lay by against future needs what *ought* to be laid out in the present necessities of God's work. They will never so far take their

---

2. A gentleman once told us that his wine bill was £100 a year—more than enough to keep a Scripture reader always at work in some populous district. And to our mind one of the countless advantages of total abstinence is, that it at once sets money free for such work. Smoking, too, is a habit not only injurious to the health in the vast majority of cases, and, to our mind, not becoming in a 'temple of the Holy Ghost,' but also one which squanders money which might be used for the Lord. Expenses in dress might in most people be curtailed. Expensive 'tastes' should be denied; and simplicity in all habits of life should mark the followers of Him who had not 'where to lay His head,' There are, however, bright examples of those who could live at large expense giving this up, and living in the simplest way, and at the least possible expense, to use more in the Lord's service.

future out of His hands by encroaching on the portion which should be given to Him.

And this is one reason why we strongly recommend it. *It is a scriptural method of exhibiting trust in God.* It is very well to talk of trust. But with some it means very little. The moment it is required to be *really* exercised, many shrink back.

Of this, however, we are sure—that not only does God, in a general way, provide for those who trust Him in a general way, but a very *manifest* and *special* blessing seems vouchsafed from the moment the believer definitely and really exercises his trust, in setting apart a *first charge* on his income for the Lord. He not only shares more largely the blessedness of the man 'that considereth the poor' (Psalm 12:1-3), in all the many forms in which it is described in God's word; but all that he thus 'lends unto the Lord,' He will 'pay him again' (Proverbs 19:17), not only hereafter when the fullest reaping time comes, but He will not keep us waiting so long. As we 'honor the Lord with our substance, and with *the first-fruits of all our increase,*' our 'barns shall be filled with plenty' (Proverbs 3:10). Only we must heartily believe and act upon His promise, which will prove true in this, as in everything else, 'Them that honor Me I will honor' (1 Samuel 2:30).

But some may ask what is to be understood by giving this special sum to the Lord. Is it all to go in actual subscriptions to Christian work, or given to the poor? We reply that it may be laid out in anything which is *distinctly a work of love to others done for the Lord's sake.* This includes a wide field for its employment.

Some may feel it such a work of love to devote something to help poorer relations, who of all have the greatest claim on us, when they really need it. Temporal blessings bestowed upon others is a work which Christ Himself did, when He 'went about doing good' (Acts 10:38); and when bestowed for His sake, and after His example, is real service for Him. As He did not confine Himself to giving spiritual blessings, neither should we, in laying out money for Him; but, like Him, we should seek to make the temporal open the way for the spiritual. Bodily comforts of all kinds for the sick, food and clothing for the poor, should certainly come out 'of the Lord's purse.' Hospitals and infirmaries should be supported from it.

Then there are countless Christian works going on which call for help. Mission agencies of every description want funds; and these we should help as liberally as we can. Medical missions especially should be helped, as uniting spiritual and temporal blessings. The Temperance cause should be well assisted. There is also the ministry and service of God in our own neighborhood which we must support, whether by pew rents, freewill contributions, or collections. Then the distribution of religious literature—books, tracts, and papers—does untold good, and should have a large share of the money. Gospel Temperance literature should also be circulated as widely as possible. Other similar channels in which to distribute available money will suggest themselves.

But we must return to our first thoughts in this chapter. After our tenth has been deducted to give to the Lord, what about the rest? It is all His, and should be spent as such. Were this really done, we believe that many who felt that they ought to devote less than a tenth would find out that they could give more than they thought. They would begin to ask themselves whether they *really want* this or that, or whether they could not just, or almost as well, do without it; and they would often discover that there was, after all, more which they could give to God than they at first supposed. Economy and care in expenditure would be the result, not, as it so often is, just because of 'limited means.' But whether the means are 'limited ' or not, the economy and care would arise from the very highest grounds—grounds that would link all expenditure with God Himself. And economy, be it remembered, is not necessarily to buy the cheapest thing, but what will give best value for the money expended, although perhaps dearest at first.

Those who try to spend all their money for God get into the habit of seeking His will as to what they ought or ought not to purchase, even in the least things. To some it may be a new thought to connect such little matters with God, or to suppose that He is interested in what we spend. But He is interested, more than we can imagine, in all that concerns His people, for it concerns Himself, with whom they (with all their interests) are one.

This habit of seeking His will should be cultivated, not in any spirit of scrupulous bondage, but with that happy willingness to please Him in everything which a really devoted child naturally exhibits towards a really beloved parent. It should be carried out in the spirit of the child who knows that his parents wish him to be happy, and to have all that is reasonably conducive to happiness, and comfort, and health.

This habit would give an untold interest to life, and do much towards establishing a frequent spirit of communion with God. It shows a very hallowing influence over ordinary life, to see that money laid out on the necessaries of existence may be regarded as spent for Him. 'Tradesmen's bills' would be looked upon in a different light, as registers of His supply of our needs, and as His provision for others to live; and they would be more readily and punctually 'settled.' Wages paid for necessary service would be regarded in the same way.

10

TIME AS A TALENT

The recognition of time as a talent for use in God's service is a most important feature in a really consecrated life. It is a most valuable treasure, and may be turned to untold account.

There are several particulars about it which it will be well to consider.

Unlike most other things usually regarded as talents, time is at the disposal of all alike. We are not speaking, now of what is called 'leisure time' only. It would be a very imperfect way of treating our subject if we confined it to that. Indeed, many lose sight of some of the deepest truths connected with it, by speaking as if only those who had such leisure time had time which could be devoted to God.[1]

This idea is entirely wrong. It would make a fanciful inequality between the service which God's people render to Him, which has no existence in fact. Moreover, it would depress many who have to work almost all day in the whirl of business and family life by the thought that they render every little service to God.

---

1. This subject is more fully dealt with in *The Consecrated Life* (published by Nisbet & Co., price 1$.), chap. iv. and v, on 'Consecration in Daily Life,' and 'Family Life.'

The fact is, that as regards time *everybody has all there is to have*. The twenty-four hours of each day are entrusted to all alike. None have more, and none less, than others. There is a perfect equality, and when the matter is rightly understood, it will be seen that none has an advantage over another in respect of time to devote to God.

Time, therefore, is a talent which *must* be used in some way by all. It is absolutely *forced* upon us. Its use is going on each hour, each moment, whether we notice it or not; and the only question with us all is as to *how* we are using it. For this reason it needs the very greatest care in its use. It slips from us almost without our knowing it. Unless we 'keep our wits about us,' or better still (and with the Christian it means the same thing), unless we 'set the Lord alway before us' (Psalm 16:8), immense portions of it will be lost.

Then as regards the value of time, too much cannot possibly be said. It will, however, not be necessary to repeat the thoughts expressed about 'Life as a talent,' in a former chapter. What is said there of life is, of course, true of time, which is only another aspect of 'life.' But we may remark the common maxim in business life, that 'Time is money.' It is the strongest idea which a worldly man can conceive.

Money with him is the highest good, and time will earn it; therefore time is money. But the Christian has far stronger reasons for thinking most highly of the value of time. In the deepest sense it 'is money' with him, his 'Lord's Money,' and he values it and uses it accordingly.

But there is, perhaps, nothing which is so manifestly a talent committed to our trust, and for the use of which we shall be answerable to God, that is less thought about or more wantonly thrown away. Even those who have a clear sense of their stewardship before God as regards many other matters, do not grasp it very closely as regards time. Many think little or nothing of wasted hours and days. Whole mornings, afternoons, and evenings frittered away cause them no trouble of conscience at all. Very many who would never willingly waste their money, waste their time without a thought.

We all need to be reminded continually that our time is not our own. We recognize ownership over time, in the human sense, in our dealings with each other. The time that is paid for belongs to the one who engages it. But we forget that, in the highest and most real sense, our time *belongs to God*. People sometimes speak of having 'time which they can call their own.' As regards our dealings with one another this expression may be allowed; but it is apt to mislead. When we view time from the highest standpoint, it has no place at all.

None really have time, any more than they have money, which they can truly say is 'their own.' Every day, every hour, every moment as it passes by, is only entrusted to us by God to use for Him. It is in no proper sense our own, but absolutely and entirely His.

If our time, then, so absolutely belongs to God, how are we entitled to use it? We answer, without any hesitation, that it must be used by us with constant reference to His will concerning it. We must spend it as we know or believe that He will approve.

This at once opens out several considerations. We shall deal first with time in general, and then with 'leisure time.'

Under the head of 'time in general' comes, of course, the everyday occupation of daily life. Every lawful calling has its place in God's providential arrangements for the well-being of mankind, and may be followed out in Him and for Him. He supplies our necessities and comforts through human means; and those who provide for or manufacture them are His agents in the world. This thought enables the believer to see that in the busiest life he may be 'doing the will of God from the heart'[2] (Ephesians 6:6). The same is true of all the necessary duties of family and home life; they may all be fulfilled as time spent for God, who has laid those duties upon us.

In spending our time for God in this general but very real sense, we would offer a few suggestions towards making the utmost use of it we can.

---

2. It should be noticed that these words are applied by St. Paul to the daily labor of the Ephesian slaves, purely 'secular work,' as people could call it. But this motive turns all that would otherwise be secular into religious work of a higher order. The reference in Colossions 3:23 is exactly the same.

Those who really believe that they are spending their time for God in their daily occupations will be very faithful and diligent in discharging them properly. They will be faithful to God about it all, when they recognize that it is His work that they are doing. But this will be no mere theory with them. They will show it by their faithfulness to those for whom they are doing it in the human sense. They will keenly watch the interests of those whom they serve, when they realize that, in the higher sense, they are God's interests also.

They will also do all they have to do, not merely because it is their duty, but heartily and willingly, just because they take it up as God's work for them in this world and their work for Him. 'Heartily, as to the Lord, and not unto men' (Colossions 3:23), will be their constant rule; and in the daily realization of it they will enjoy the work which otherwise might be a source of weariness and toil. To be tired out in *His* service is a very different thing from feeling wearied with what we have only regarded as drudgery for man's sake.

Then this heartiness in taking up our work is the secret of *thoroughness* in doing it. 'With thy might' (Ecclesiastes 9:10), is the secret of a really successful worker. When work, whatever it be, is not thoroughly done, a waste of time results. But to do anything thoroughly, our will must be put into it; and we shall never put our will into any work which is not in itself very agreeable to flesh and blood, until we take it up with a consecrated will, as what God would have us do.

Some further remarks are necessary on the use of time, more especially for those whose general daily occupation is not confined to settled work during fixed hours. Many have plenty to do, but no time absolutely fixed for them by others which must be spent upon it. These are in special danger of wasting time.

Our first advice under these circumstances is, as far as possible, to *fix for themselves* a time for each work, and to do their best to keep to it. Regularity and habit have a great deal to do with the best use of time. What is left to any time is often left undone altogether; or else either too much time is devoted to it, which means waste of time, or (what is just as bad) too little time for doing it properly is bestowed upon it, which means that it is not done as it should be.

There is a great secret in the *management* of time. Some do so much more with their time than others. It is generally noticed that those who do the most are usually the readiest to take on something more. It is because they have learned the habit of managing their time. They do not work at haphazard, but arrange their time according to what they have to do. No one should plead that they have 'no time' for one thing or another until they have thus laid out their time, and found that it really is so. Too often the answer of 'no time for it,' whether about taking up new work, or not doing what really lies in our way, is a simple untruth.[3]

There is a great deal more in the common expression 'to make time' for a thing than people often think. There is a sense in which time can be made. It is a well-known maxim about money, that '*money saved* is money made.' It is very true; but it is equally true of time. Many make a great deal of time for what others leave undone 'for want of time,' by saving time here and there, which others allow to pass by unused.

The great secret for saving time is to *look after the minutes*. Here another worldly maxim helps us : 'Take care of the pence, and the pounds will take care of themselves.' We say, 'Take care of the minutes, and the hours and days will take care of themselves.' Few realize the value of' spare minutes.' Every five minutes in a day saved, which might otherwise be wasted, means, if we omit the Sundays, just half-an-hour a week, which is 26 hours, or ignore than two working days of 12 hours each, during the year. Let each calculate how many working days of 12 hours each they could not thus 'make' by saving and using well the 'only five minutes' which they little regard.

One important way of saving time is to have 'a place for everything,' and then to see (which is something far more than this)

---

3. How often people tell their friends that they have had 'no time to write to them before,' when it simply means that they have not cared to be at the trouble of doing it!

that everything is in its place.' The minutes lost in hunting for what cannot be found would often thus be saved for better use.

Another way of making time is *to rise early*. Many waste several 'five minutes' every day by a habit, injurious to the health as well as to one's general character and usefulness, by lying dozing in bed in the morning.

A word of caution, however, is necessary about apparent methods of trying to save time which are not really so.

There is the health-destroying habit of staying up late at night. Some can do better work at night, or think that they can; and they yield to the temptation. But it must sooner or later tell on the general health. Sleep is as much our duty before God as anything else can possibly be. Time spent on it, in proper measure, is not wasted, but used in the highest sense in His service. To shorten it is to sin against His law for our well-being, which is to sin against Him. No time is perhaps so truly wasted, however much we may have to show for it, as that which is taken from sleeping time.

Again, time is not saved by doing things in a hurry. 'The more haste, the less speed,' is a true saying. To be *quick* is a thing to be cultivated; but this does not mean to be *hurried*.

What is done hurriedly is rarely done well, and often has to be done over again; and even if it is well done, injury results to the general health, from crowding into a given time more than can properly be done in it. To take *time enough* for everything, and yet not too much, should be the aim of all who want to use their time to the best advantage.

Once more, no time is really saved by trying to do two things at once. One thing should be done at a time, and the undivided attention given to it, if it is to be done so as best to use the time devoted to it. Those who try to do more than one thing at a time do neither really well, and also put a strain upon the mental powers which is sure to make itself felt in time.

Two very fruitful methods of wasting time must now be noticed. They are unfortunately very common, and call for a word of warning.

Some people indulge largely in what are called 'daydreams,' or 'building castles in the air.' They let their imagination work unchecked as to what they should like to be or to do, or what they fear may happen, until it all seems for the time like a present reality which is actually taking place. In this dreamy condition they spend much time by day which might be otherwise usefully employed; or, if at night, they rob themselves of necessary sleep. But not only is time so spent thoroughly wasted, but an injury is done to the mind itself, and a habit is formed which has a ruinous effect on the general character. 'Dreamy' people are very trying to deal with.

Others waste much time, and also impair their mental powers, by indulging in *after regrets*. They worry themselves that things did not happen differently, and picture to their minds how it would have been had they turned out differently, till they get into an unreal and therefore mentally and spiritually an unhealthy condition. One great secret of usefully employing time is to live in the present moment, and to throw oneself heartily into its work.

We should use the past, not as a matter for vain regrets that it was not different, but just to profit by its experience. As regards the future, we should use proper means of provision for it, but leave its actual circumstances trustfully in God's hands. But the present moment is what is always before us to misuse or to lay out to advantage; and that, with whatever occupation it brings, should have our undivided attention.

We now come to speak of what is generally called 'leisure time'—time, that is, which we are not obliged to occupy with the absolutely necessary duties of life, and which we can dispose of in any way which we prefer. Some have more and some less, and some again hardly any; but of very few indeed could it be truly said that they have none at all.

The question arises, How is this to be used? We answer again, with constant reference to the will of God. In further explanation of this we offer a few remarks which we hope may be of use to many.

Let none doubt that time devoted, within proper limits, to innocent and healthy recreation, is spent in the service of God. Nay; it is an absolute duty which He has laid upon us by those laws of nature with which He has surrounded our being, and which we cannot disobey without disobedience to Him and suffering to ourselves. Indeed, we go so far as to say that time devoted to work of any kind which ought to be given to recreation or rest of mind and body is wasted in the fullest sense of the word. Only let us see that our recreation is, as the word itself means, confined to what will really recreate or renew our wearied energies, and does not involve excitement of mind, late hours, or anything unbecoming a Christian who desires to seek God's glory in this as in everything else.

Moreover, in family life it becomes the duty of some to devote time in ministering to the needful recreation of others. Some members of the family may work hard during the day in professional, business, or school life, and naturally look to the others, and specially, perhaps, to the sisters, to join them in their recreations in the evenings. To do so, under such circumstances, is to fulfill a service to God; and with this motive in view, such time may be reckoned as spent for Him. Those, however, who can arrange their own time will, of course, do so that this time may fall in with their own recreation time also; and thus they will make a double use of their time.

But as with money, so also, we think, with time, that a certain proportion, and, if possible, a fixed one, should be devoted more specially to definite work for God. This work may take various forms, such as any sort of evangelistic work; visiting the sick and poor; teaching the ignorant; comforting the afflicted; writing for God, as suggested in the chapter on *The Consecrated Pen*; making garments for the needy, or anything which may be sold for the Lord's work,[4] and anything else of the same sort. This devotion of time to God is most important, for it means personal service to Him. So many give their money to further God's work, and think that it is all they need do. They give to enable others to do personal work for God, but they do next to none themselves. Personal service, however, in some active work for God, is the duty and privilege of

---

4. Much of this 'making' could be done of an evening when the family generally meets for recreation and conversation; also in this way many spare 'five minutes,' here and there, could be saved during the day and used to advantage.

all who have health and strength for it, and no giving of money can take its place.

Moreover, time devoted to God's service is a good substitute for money, when there is very little money to give. Money may be made in many ways for this purpose by those who have time to do so. But the devotion of time to definite spiritual work for souls is a far more direct way of using one's time for God than trying to earn money by it to set others to do the spiritual work.

Lastly, we think it right to say a word about wasting other *people's time*. Many do this without a thought. They are not punctual to an engagement, coming too late, or (what is sometimes almost as bad) too soon. They keep visitors waiting long in their drawing-rooms, before they come to them. They do not keep to the regular hours of the household arrangements. They dawdle without need over a purchase, an interview, or a meal. They mislay their things, and others have to look for them. They are 'an age' getting ready to go out, while others are waiting for them. If they are servants, they are late with the meals; they are irregular in 'doing rooms' upon which others depend; or they are long in answering the door, or the house bells, which means that others are kept waiting.

Many other ways will occur to all who think about it. But of them all we would say, that if it is wrong to waste our own time, it is even still more culpable to waste that of other people. Let us see that the time of others is to some extent in our power, and that, since it is the 'Lord's Money' as much as our own time is, it must not be diverted from its rightful employment by others in His service and work, through any negligence or thoughtlessness on our part.

www.ingramcontent.com/pod-product-compliance
Lightning Source LLC
Chambersburg PA
CBHW050041080526
44586CB00014B/1405